Monitoring poverty and social exclusion in Scotland

■ Peter Kenway, Steven Fuller, Mohibur Rahman, Cathy Street and Guy Palmer

poverty.org.uk

JOSEPH
ROWNTREE
FOUNDATION

Crown Copyright is reproduced with permission from the Controller of Her Majesty's Stationery Office.

The LFS data used in this report was made available through the ESRC Data Archive. The data was collected by the ESRC Research Centre on Micro Social Change at the University of Essex. Neither the original collectors of the data nor the Archive bear any responsibility for the analyses presented here.

The same applies for all datasets used in this report, including those from the Department for Education and Skills, the Department for Work and Pensions, the General Register Office for Scotland, the Scottish Executive, and the Office for National Statistics.

The **Joseph Rowntree Foundation** has supported this project as part of its programme of research and innovative development projects, which it hopes will be of value to policy makers, practitioners and service users. The facts presented and views expressed in this report are, however, those of the authors and not necessarily those of the Foundation.

Published by
Joseph Rowntree Foundation
The Homestead
40 Water End
York YO30 6WP
Website: www.jrf.org.uk

© New Policy Institute 2002

First published 2002 by the Joseph Rowntree Foundation

ISBN 1 85935 076 3 (paperback)
       1 85935 077 1 (pdf: available at www.jrf.org.uk)

A CIP catalogue record for this report is available from the British Library.

Contents

3 Ill health   71

4 Quality of life and social cohesion   89

Acknowledgements

This report has involved extensive collaboration with many people and organisations in Scotland and throughout Great Britain. We have benefited greatly from their help and advice.

We would like to thank members of the advisory group convened by the Joseph Rowntree Foundation for helping steer this project and for their detailed comments on the drafts. Thanks go to Neil McIntosh, Scotland Advisor to the Joseph Rowntree Foundation; Glen Bramley, Heriot-Watt University and the Centre for Research into Socially Inclusive Services; Mary Duffy, Health Education Board for Scotland; Robina Goodlad, Glasgow University and the Scottish Centre for Research on Social Justice; Peter Kelly, Poverty Alliance; Steven Maxwell, Scottish Council for Voluntary Organisations; Jim McCormick, Scottish Council Foundation; Richard Mitchell, Edinburgh University; Gina Netto, Scottish Ethnic Minority Research Unit, Heriot-Watt University; and Cathy Sharp, Communities Scotland.

We are also grateful to a number of people whose expert guidance and suggestion has proved invaluable. They include Graham Atherton, CoSLA; Nick Bailey, Glasgow University and the Scottish Centre for Research on Social Justice; Mark Batho, Head of the Social Justice Group at the Scottish Executive; Usha Brown, Scottish Poverty Information Unit, Glasgow Caledonian University; Stephen Curtis and Simon Wakefield, Scottish Parliament Information Centre; David Donnison and Ken Judge, Glasgow University; Phil Hanlon, the Public Health Institute of Scotland; Damian Killeen, Poverty Alliance; Barbara Knowles, Falkirk Council; Fiona Montgomery, Linda Rosborough and Peter Whitehouse, Scottish Executive; Stephen Platt, Edinburgh University; Danny Phillips, Child Poverty Action Group, Scotland; Bill Scott, Lothian Anti Poverty Alliance; Gill Scott, Scottish Poverty Information Unit and Glasgow Caledonian University; Mark Shucksmith, the Arkleton Centre For Rural Development Research, Aberdeen University and the Scottish Centre for Research on Social Justice; Kay Tisdall, Children in Scotland; David Webster, Housing Department, Glasgow City Council; Daniel Wight, Medical Research Council, Scotland; and Gillian Young, Communities Scotland.

The report would not have been possible without the assistance in supplying the data by a large number of civil service statisticians in the Scottish Executive, the General Register Office for Scotland, the Office for National Statistics and the Department for Work and Pensions. In particular we would like to thank Colin Wilkie-Jones from Households Below Average Income at DWP and the team at the Central Statistics Unit (Scottish Household Survey) at the Scottish Executive for their detailed and comprehensive comments on drafts of the indicators.

We would like to thank colleagues at the New Policy Institute who helped on this project: Luke Dickson, James Gledhill and Naomi Parsons.

This project would not have been possible without the material and intellectual help and support provided by the Joseph Rowntree Foundation. We would like to thank Derek Williams helping us manage the project and for his innumerable comments on ideas and drafts throughout, Danielle Walker whose considerable support and encouragement helped start this project and Donald Hirsch for his detailed comments on the indicators. Finally, we would like to thank Alison Elks for her patient assistance in putting the report together under a very tight schedule.

As ever, responsibility for the report, including the errors within it, belongs to the authors alone.

Executive summary

Introduction

This report contains an independent selection of graphs, maps and commentary that together present a picture of poverty, inequality and social exclusion in Scotland. Its focus throughout is both on aggregate progress in Scotland over time as well as differences within Scotland, whether by social class, age, gender, or local authority area, or between rural and urban areas.

The report is an offspring of *Monitoring Poverty and Social Exclusion*, an annual report which, since 1998, has provided an independent record of the progress on poverty and exclusion across Great Britain. The affinity between this report and the British one is clear. In particular, without claiming to be comprehensive, both range widely in their choice of subjects, covering such diverse matters as income, education, health, and the neighbourhood or local area where people live.

The report is, though, not just a replica of the British one, having been built up from scratch to reflect the particular concerns that were expressed by people we consulted in Scotland during its construction. They include the need to:

▌ pay attention to the economic factors behind poverty, inequality and exclusion, as well as the outcomes;

▌ look beneath the figures for the country as a whole by drawing attention to variations between different areas within Scotland; and

▌ cover subjects reserved to the UK government as well as those devolved to the Scottish Executive.

Although the report compares Scotland with England and Wales, usually in the text but sometimes in a graph too, this is not one of its main aims. Such comparisons are therefore occasional and are only made where there is a point of significant interest.

The report is organised into four chapters containing a total of 34 indicators and 6 maps. The four chapters are: poverty and low income; employment and education; ill health; and quality of life and social cohesion. Each indicator occupies a separate page and is made up of two graphs, one usually measuring progress over time and the second providing a breakdown of the statistic across Scotland. Each indicator is also supported by text which provides technical information explaining the indicator and offering an assessment of its reliability. Five of the indicators also have associated maps (and there is also one map that is not associated with an indicator).

Each chapter includes a contribution written by an invited expert based in Scotland on a subject connected with the chapter (the final chapter containing two such contributions). While these articles naturally vary in style and content, each is aiming to answer the same question, namely, how we will be able to tell in a number of years' time whether there has been real progress or not. An appendix to the report provides a summary of the relevant policies, detailing the main policy initiatives under way and whether responsibility for them is reserved to Westminster or devolved to Holyrood.

What the indicators show

Up to 2000/01, there was no sign of a fall in the number of people on relative low income...

Over the four years 1997/98 to 2000/01, the proportion of people in Scotland below the official, relative low income threshold rose slightly, from 21^1/$_2$ to 23^1/$_2$ per cent; that is, 1.2 million people on a low income in 2000/01 [1a]. Over the same period, the proportion of children (just under 30 per cent) in such households barely altered, implying some 310,000 children in low income households in 2000/01 (the latest year for which data is available) [2a]. Over the seven year period for which there is reliable data, the overall sense is one of little change, the average proportion on low income in 1998/99 to 2000/01 being identical to that for 1994/95 to 1996/97 [1a].

...but beneath the surface there is change, with unemployment falling and low income in work becoming more prevalent...

Thanks to falling unemployment, down from 8 per cent of the working age population in 1994 to 6 per cent in 2000 [13a], there was a fall in the number of low income, working age households who are unemployed. The share they represent of all low income households also fell, down from 25 per cent over the period 1994/95 to 1996/97, to 19 per cent over the 1998/99 to 2000/01 period.

By contrast, there was a rise in the number of low income households containing someone who is working, these 'working poor' households accounting for 41 per cent of the low income, working age households in the period 1998/99 to 2000/01 [8b]. One factor that is likely to be related to this is the growth, slow but nevertheless steady, in the inequality of earnings among men (although not among women) over at least the last decade. [17a]

...and with benefits, though rising in real terms, still leaving people solely reliant on them far short of the relative low income threshold

Thanks to a variety of changes in the tax and benefit system, some low incomes have risen in real terms, thereby sharply reducing the number of people below an absolute low income threshold [1a]. Even so, some people who are solely reliant on means-tested benefits, for example couples whether with children or not, were still more than £60 a week short of the relative low income threshold at the end of 2000 [6b].

Recent, more partial evidence provides conflicting pointers to the way the situation will have moved on in the last 18 months. On the positive side...

The low income numbers for 2000/01 pre-date the big rise in the pensioners' Minimum Income Guarantee – from £78 to £92 for a single pensioner and from £122 to £141 for a pensioner couple – which took effect in April 2001. The downward movement in the proportion of pensioners that was visible in 2000/01 [2a] is therefore likely to continue in 2001/02. In addition, the take-up of the Working Families Tax Credit, which was introduced in October 1999, is still continuing to rise [15a].

...but these are at least partially offset by a mixed employment situation...

Over the two years from spring 2000, a period when the total number of jobs in Scotland was growing, the number of jobs in industry (manufacturing, energy, water and mining), construction and agriculture, fell by some 10 per cent [16a]. In view of the importance of having two-earner households to escape from low income [8a], the loss of such predominantly male, manual jobs may be disproportionately important. Even during the five years to 2000, when the total number of jobs in these sectors remained broadly unchanged, several local authority districts lost more than 10 per cent of their jobs in these sectors [16b].

...and there remain some deep-seated and long-standing problems where progress is slow or non-existent

Over the four years to 2001, there was a barely perceptible fall in the 340,000 working age people who had been claiming one of the key social security benefits for two years or more [7a], four-fifths of whom were sick or disabled [7b]. In spring 2002, nearly 210,000 working age households had been without work for three years or more, the highest number for at least a decade [14a]. A high and rising proportion of unemployed people are only able to find short-term work, 45 per cent of those making a new claim for Jobseeker's Allowance in spring 2002 having last claimed the benefit less than six months previously [18a].

There are signs of progress within the education system...

Standard Grade attainment continued to climb through to 2001, both on average and for the weakest fifth of students [10a]. The proportion of school leavers whose highest qualification is a Standard Grade 1 or 2 has risen sharply over the past five years, from 16 to 24 per cent, with a corresponding fall in the proportion getting nothing higher than a Standard Grade 3 or 4 [11a]. The proportion going into further or higher education also rose, to above 50 per cent in 2000/01 from 40 per cent a decade earlier [12a].

...but the gap in attainment remains considerable, with only slight improvements at the bottom...

The gap in attainment at Standard Grade between the bottom 20 per cent and the average is still large and shows no convincing sign of reducing [10a]. There has also been no reduction since 1998/99 in the number leaving school with either nothing, or nothing better than the lowest Standard Grades (5 or 6), some 5,000 school leavers in 2000/01 [11a]. In spring 2000, around a fifth of all 19-year-olds – some 13,000 people – had no qualification (including vocational qualifications) higher than an SVQ2 or equivalent, a proportion no different from 1996, although the trend since 2000 has been downward [10b].

...and from the point of view of the individual, there are real risks here

The fewer the qualifications a person has the higher their risk of unemployment, ranging from 4 per cent for those with higher education, to 10 per cent for those with no more than Standard Grades, to 13 per cent for those with no qualifications [9a]. Unemployment remains high among young adults, especially men, with around 1 in 7 of those aged 18 to 25 unemployed in spring 2002 [9b]. This is associated with further risks: 80 per cent of all 15- to 24-year-olds who commence a spell of treatment for drug misuse are unemployed, including one-sixth who have *never* been employed [25b].

Scotland is making progress in cutting its high rates of premature death...

For men aged 65, the death rate was more than a fifth lower in 2000 than it had been a decade earlier, with most of the improvement coming in the last five years [20a]. A fall of such a magnitude, which is broadly typical of death rates for men throughout their 60s, is clearly very positive.

...but the inequalities within Scotland remain substantial...

Standardised Mortality Rates in the 10 per cent most deprived local areas were more than twice as high as in the 50 per cent least deprived local areas [20b], while for stomach cancer, lung cancer and heart disease, the rates in 2000 for the worst two local authority areas were more than 30 per cent above average [23b]. The incidence of self-reported long-standing illness or disability is markedly higher among those in social rented accommodation, with 1 in 5 of those aged under 45 and almost 1 in 2 of those aged 45 to 60 reporting the condition [21b].

...while some problems persist

There have been around 120 suicides among young adults aged 15 to 24 each year over the last decade, there being no sign of a fall here [24a] nor in the death rate from all causes for 25-year-olds [20a]. Some 1,300 underweight babies were born in 2001, low birth weight being a signifier of likely health problems in later life [22a]. The proportion this represents (2^1/$_2$ per cent) remained unchanged over the previous decade.

The halving in just four years of the number of homes without central heating is very positive ...

In 1999/00, the proportion of homes without central heating had fallen to 8 per cent, from 17 per cent four years earlier. For homes with low income, the proportion also halved, from 25 to 13 per cent [28a]. This development is doubly good, not only for its effect on health but also because of the lower running costs associated with a more efficient heating system.

...but homelessness remains a persistent and growing problem

Some 34,000 households were deemed to be homeless in 1999/00, a number that increased over the 1990s [26a]. Despite the stock of properties in the social rented sector falling by a quarter (reflecting right-to-buy sales) during the 1990s, it is not obvious that the availability of affordable housing has got any worse, with the number of new lets each year remaining broadly constant over the 1990s [27a].

Finally, particular groups face disproportionate problems...

More people from manual backgrounds than people from non-manual backgrounds are dissatisfied with the quality of the services provided by their local council [29a]. The feeling that it is very unsafe to walk alone in one's local area at night is held more often by those from manual backgrounds than those from professional or other non-manual backgrounds [32b]. Almost half of those in rural areas find public transport inconvenient, compared with 1 in 10 in urban areas and 1 in 6 in small rural towns [30a].

...including some that are long-standing, well-known and the subject of official attention

The proportion of low income households without any kind of bank or building society account remained at around 30 per cent, equivalent to some 130,000 households in 2000/01, a level it had been at since 1994/95. By contrast, the proportion for the population as a whole has remained at under 10 per cent [31a]. Only 1 in 5 people in urban areas feel involved in their local community, compared with 2 in 5 for those living in rural areas [33a]. The decline in the turnout for the 2001 General Election compared with four years earlier was proportionately highest in those constituencies where turnout had been lowest to start with [34a].

Conclusion

There are two, general conclusions that we draw from our analysis. The first is the stubborn refusal of so many of the key measures of poverty and exclusion in Scotland to show any signs of movement. With the exception of one of the education statistics, all of the numbers in the table below are – at best – no lower at the end of our period of measurement than they were at the beginning.

Second, a strategy to reduce poverty that is built on getting people into work faces a serious challenge when 40 per cent of the working age poor are actually already in work. To the extent that the alleviation of 'in work' poverty depends on the system of tax credits and minimum wage, it is a UK matter at least in the first instance, especially since the problem is no worse in Scotland than elsewhere. Where perhaps Scotland does stand out, however, is in the very high proportion of its economically inactive who are sick and disabled. Since people in this position are not expected to work, the question of how they are to escape from low income and poverty is one that at the moment is without an answer.

Up to date statistics

All indicators used in this report are available on the NPI website (www.poverty.org.uk).

Ten key statistics

1,200,000	people of all ages living in low income households (2000/01)
340,000	working age people claiming benefits for 2+ years (2001)
310,000	children living in low income households (2000/01)
210,000	working age households without work for 3+ years (2002)
130,000	households in the poorest fifth lacking any bank account, etc. (2000/01)
34,000	households deemed to be homeless (1999/00)
13,000	19-year-olds with no qualification better than an SVQ2 or equivalent (2002)
5,000	school leavers with no more than Standard Grade 5/6 (2000/01)
1,300	low birth-weight babies (2001)
120	young adult suicides (2001)

Summary of the indicators: performance over 5 years

Indicator	Over 5 years
Poverty and low income	
1 All individuals with low income	Steady
2 Children and pensioners with low income	Steady
3 Intensity of low income	Steady
4 Inequality in Scotland	Worsened
5 Spread of low income	Steady
6 Working age people in receipt of benefit	Improved
7 On long-term benefit	Steady
Employment and education	
8 Risk of low income	Worsened
9 Risk of unemployment	N/A
10 Low attainment at school	Steady
11 Qualifications of school leavers	Improved
12 Destination of school leavers	Improved
13 Economic status of those of working age	Improved
14 Households without work for two years or more	Steady
15 In receipt of Working Families Tax Credit	Improved
16 Blue-collar employment	Worsened
17 Low pay and pay inequalities	Worsened
18 Insecure at work	Steady
19 Without access to training	Steady
Ill health	
20 Death rates for those aged 25 and 65	Improved
21 Long-standing illness or disability	N/A
22 Low birth-weight babies	Steady
23 Standardised mortality rates for three diseases	Steady
24 Suicides	Steady
25 Problem drug use	Steady
Quality of life and social cohesion	
26 Homeless households	Worsened
27 Affordable housing	Steady
28 Households without central heating	Improved
29 Satisfaction with services	N/A
30 Satisfaction with public transport	N/A
31 Without a bank or building society account	Steady
32 Satisfaction with local area	N/A
33 Participation in the community	N/A
34 Voting	Worsened

Introduction

Why this report

This report is an offspring of *Monitoring Poverty and Social Exclusion*, an annual report which, since 1998, has provided an independent record of the progress being made in combating poverty and social exclusion across Great Britain. This report, exclusively for Scotland, has been produced following extensive consultation with a wide range of people during 2001 and early 2002, both as to whether such a report would be of value, and what its focus should be.

The affinity between this report and the British one is clear. In particular, without claiming to be comprehensive, both range widely in their choice of subjects, covering such diverse matters as income, education, health and the state of the neighbourhood. Some indicators of progress are common to both, especially those on low income. But this report is far from being a replica of the British one, reflecting the fact that the circumstances in 2002 in Scotland are different in a number of ways from those in 1998 in Britain as a whole.[1]

As a result, and despite its clear roots, the selection of indicators in this report has been built up from scratch in an attempt to reflect the particular concerns and angles that were emphasised to us in our consultations. They are:

■ Besides measuring the extent of problems and the effect of policies to alleviate them, there is a need to pay attention to **the economic factors that cause and reinforce poverty, inequality and exclusion**. In response, the report includes a larger set of indicators on aspects of work and jobs, as well as giving a higher priority to housing.

■ There is a need to look behind figures for the country as a whole by drawing attention to **variations between different areas within Scotland**, including highlighting problems of special significance in rural areas. Responding to this concern is a major theme of this report, achieved by means of several maps showing the situation for the 32 different local authorities in Scotland, and by providing breakdowns of several indicators according to a six part classification of the country into different types of urban or rural area.

■ There is a need to cover **subjects reserved to the UK government** as well as those devolved to the Scottish Executive, in particular, low income and the tax and benefit system more generally. This is an acknowledgement of the interdependence of UK and Scottish policy-making in tackling poverty and social exclusion.[2]

■ We should avoid a common weakness of indicator reports, namely failing properly to reflect **popular and community concerns**.[3] Although the research for this report did not include any widespread or systematic survey, by drawing on the results of one such study and using data from the new, annual Scottish Household Survey, the report begins to show what is possible here, with several indicators devoted to community-inspired notions of 'well-being'.

■ It is important to look at issues facing ***people from ethnic minorities***, which are at least as difficult as elsewhere in Britain, but tend to be overlooked both because the population is relatively small and because the data available is usually very limited. Although the data is too thin to allow any minority ethnic graphs to be drawn, where reliable data has been found, a point has been made in the accompanying commentary.

■ It is important to go beyond the ***Social Justice Annual Report***. Of the 68 graphs included here, only around one-quarter appear in the 2001 edition of the official report. Two factors account for this small degree of overlap: first, the emphasis given here to the geographical and socio-economic breakdowns of indicators, as well as the maps, and second, the attention that is given to subjects that are reserved by Westminster (e.g. tax and benefits) as well as those devolved to Holyrood.

Although the report does of course compare Scotland with England and Wales, usually in the text but sometimes in a graph too, such comparisons are occasional and are only made where there is a point of significant interest. By contrast, comparisons *within* Scotland occur much more frequently, reflecting the importance that has been attached to highlighting these variations, whether by area, class, age, gender, and so on.

Layout of the report

The report is organised into four chapters containing a total of ***34 indicators*** and ***6 maps***. After beginning with a presentation of the extent of low income, the report moves, via a consideration of some of the causal factors in education and employment, to an analysis of various inequalities of outcome across a range of domains, especially ill health, housing and access to essential services.

The primacy accorded here to education and employment does not deny the existence or importance of causes which 'run the other way' – for example, from poor housing to educational outcomes. The reason for doing it this way, however, is to try to correct what we believe to be an imbalance in other analyses of poverty and social exclusion, including official ones, which tend to overlook the extent to which 'economic' factors to do with employment influence the 'social' problems of poverty and exclusion.

The four chapters are:

1 ***Poverty and low income*** (7 indicators and 2 maps): a detailed presentation of the extent of low income, those economic and family groups most at risk, and an analysis of the geographical concentration of low income.

2 ***Employment and education*** (12 indicators and 2 maps): focusing on the causes of poverty and low income, presenting risk factors, the impact of the education system, employers' behaviour, and the effect of policy initiatives to encourage work.

3 ***Ill health*** (6 indicators and 1 map): focusing especially on inequalities in death and disease as well as factors associated with lasting disadvantage among both children and young adults.

4 ***Quality of life and social cohesion*** (9 indicators and 1 map), focusing on housing and the quality and accessibility of both public and private services, as well as people's attitudes towards, and involvement in the community.

The material within each chapter is organised around a series of *themes*, each containing between one and three (typically two) indicators. The accompanying thematic discussions cover four subjects: first, the significance of the theme; second, a description of, and justification for, the particular indicators selected; third, the key points that emerge from the accompanying indicators; and, finally, a selection of relevant key points from other sources.

Each *indicator* occupies a separate page and is made up of two graphs; the upper graph is referred to in the discussion as 'a', the lower graph as 'b'. One graph usually measures progress over time – ten years if data is available for that long – and a second, supporting graph provides a breakdown of the main statistic, for example by social class, family type, type of employment or geography (using a six-category urban–rural classification of Scotland). Where no time-series graph is provided, this is due to data limitations; this problem applies especially in Chapter 4, where there are only two years' worth of observations for graphs sourced from the Scottish Household Survey. Each indicator is also supported by text which provides technical information explaining the indicator and offering an assessment of its reliability.

Some of the indicators also have associated *maps* (and there is also one map that is not associated with an indicator). These are drawn either for the 32 local authorities or, in one case, for the 72 UK parliamentary constituencies.

Each chapter also includes a contribution *written by an invited expert* based in Scotland on a subject connected with the chapter (the final chapter containing two such contributions). While these contributions naturally vary in style and content, each is aiming to answer the same question, namely, how we will tell in a number of years' time whether there has been real progress or not.

Finally, an appendix to the report provides *a summary of the relevant policies*, detailing the main policy initiatives under way connected with the principal themes of the chapter, indicating whether the responsibility is reserved or devolved, which agency is taking the lead and what the key targets are. These policy summaries cover both the UK Government and the Scottish Executive.

Gaps in the data

In compiling this report, we have naturally become very aware of where there are gaps and shortcomings in the data that is needed on this subject, not just by independent researchers but by government and public bodies at all levels too. In some cases, this is just a matter of timing, for example, results from a new house conditions survey will be available in 2003. However, we would highlight the following subjects as being in need of attention.

Income

∎ Data on the extent of low income at the local authority level and below.

∎ Data allowing measurement of the extent to which people on low income remain on low income for a long period of time.

Housing

▮ The quantity and availability of housing, by tenure, at the level of the ward or the postcode sector.

▮ Data on investment in new housing, in both the social and private sectors.

Ill health and disability

▮ A general lack of data on people with disabilities.

▮ A general lack of data on mental health.

▮ A general lack of data on the drug problems of children, including children whose parents are misusing drugs.

Ethnic minorities

▮ A general lack of data on outcomes for ethnic minorities, including in administrative data (for example, education) where small sample size is not an issue.

The Labour Force Survey

▮ The unreliability of the Labour Force Survey at local authority level, but also possibly for various subgroups of the population within Scotland.

▮ The lack of published, reliable data on the numbers on low rates of pay.

Chapter 1 Poverty and low income

Theme	Indicator/map
Individuals on low income	Indicator 1: All individuals with low income
	Indicator 2: Children and pensioners with low income
Income inequality	Indicator 3: Intensity of low income
	Indicator 4: Inequality in Scotland
Geography: The pattern of low income	Map A: Concentration of low income
	Map B: Spread of low income
	Indicator 5: Spread of low income
Benefit dependency among working age people	Indicator 6: Working age people in receipt of benefit
	Indicator 7: Long-term receipt of benefits

Individuals on low income

In any highly developed country, low income is at the heart of the problems of poverty. Of course, an individual's income this week, this month, or even this year, does not fully determine their well-being. But the way in which British society has become ever more dominated by material goods and market relationships over the past 25 years means that a shortage of money is a greater handicap than ever. Moreover, the heightened risk of ill health and other adverse outcomes that are associated with low income, as well as the fact that around double the number of British people suffer from relative low income now compared with 20 years ago,[1] means that low income must be dealt with directly, as well as indirectly.

The chief weapons that have been used in the assault on low income over the last few years are first, reforms to the tax and benefit system and second, the national minimum wage. To the extent that responsibility for these remains with London, changes in the number of people on low income in Scotland therefore reflect the effects of British rather than Scottish policies – although Scottish-based institutions have a key role to play in implementing them.

Topics and indicators

The two indicators here provide a number of different measures of the extent of low income in Scotland and how it has changed over recent years. They are:

▍ The proportion of people in Scotland on (a) relative and (b) absolute low income.

▍ The proportion of children and pensioners with relative low income.

The first indicator [1a] shows **the proportion of people on relative low income** (defined as **the proportion of people with incomes below 60 per cent of the median household income in the current year**).[2] The choice of a *relative* measure reflects the view that the essence of poverty is about not being able to live to a standard of living that is considered to be the norm in a society at a particular time. When interpreting changes over time, it is also necessary to pay attention to the numbers on absolute low income (**the proportion with incomes below 60 per cent of the 1994/95**[3] **British median household income**),[4] which is also shown on the graph.

The supporting graph for the first indicator [1b] shows **the proportion of households lacking one or more items deemed 'essential'**, namely a telephone, a fridge or freezer, or a washing machine.[5]

Indicator 2a shows **the proportions of children**[6] **and pensioners on relative low income** (defined as **the proportion below 60 per cent of the median household income in the current year**). These two groups have been picked out because they are both the subject of major UK government policy initiatives and are also priorities within Scottish policy. In addition, the UK government's 'headline' commitments on poverty explicitly focus on child poverty, notably to abolish it within 20 years and, more specifically, to reduce it by a quarter by 2004/05.[7]

Indicator 2b shows the **distribution of children and pensioners in terms of the amount of money by which their households fall short of the low income threshold** in the most recent year (2000/01).

What the indicators show

▌ After allowing for the statistical variation that can arise in data drawn from sample surveys, there was little change in the proportion of people in Scotland on relative low income between the mid-1990s and 2000/01. For the four most recent years, however, there has been a clear, albeit slight, upward trend. [1a]

▌ By contrast, the percentage of people on absolute low income fell sharply in the two most recent years. [1a] This fall signifies that the real income (that is, after allowing for inflation) of some people with low income has risen since 1999. These real rises, however, have not been sufficiently large compared with the rise in average incomes, or sufficiently widespread, to lead to a fall in the percentage of people on relative low income.

▌ Among households where nobody is working, around 20 per cent lack one or more of the three essential items (washing machine, fridge and telephone). [1b]

▌ The proportions of both children and pensioners with relative low income showed little change over the four years to 2000/01 (it being too soon to draw any conclusions from the drop in the pensioner figure for the latest year). The proportion of children with relative low income is about 7 percentage points higher than for the population as a whole, while the proportion of pensioners below the threshold is very similar to the rate for the total population.

▌ There is a marked difference in the extent to which households with children and pensioner households fell short of 60 per cent of median income in 2000/01.[8] Thus, among low income households with children, one-tenth fell short by less than £10 a week while two-fifths fell short by more than £50 a week; among pensioners, by contrast, two-fifths fell short by less than £10 a week and one-tenth fell short by more than £50 a week.[9]

Other key points and relevant research

▌ For Britain as a whole, the proportion of people on relative low income fell from 25 to 23 per cent from 1996/97 to 2000/01 while the proportion of children in low income households fell from 34 to 30 per cent.

▌ Taking the four years 1997/98 to 2000/01 together, the proportion of minority ethnic people in low income households in Scotland is around double the rate for the population as a whole: a little under a half of minority ethnic people compared with a little under a quarter of all people in Scotland. The fact that this estimate is based on a small number of minority ethnic households means that it is subject to an unusually large degree of statistical uncertainty. The basic conclusion is, however, robust even in the presence of this uncertainty.[10]

All individuals with low income

Indicator
1

The proportion of people in households with relative low incomes has been rising gently since 1997/98. In contrast, the proportion below a fixed income threshold has been falling.

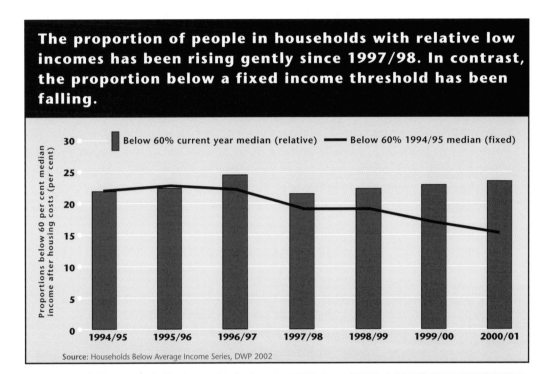

Source: Households Below Average Income Series, DWP 2002

Around a fifth of all households where the highest income householder is not working lacks a washing machine, a fridge or a telephone.

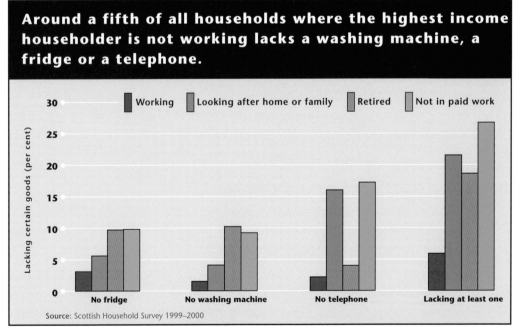

Source: Scottish Household Survey 1999–2000

The first graph shows the number of people below 60 per cent of GB median income for years since 1994/95 – the earliest year that this data is available. Two measures are shown, corresponding to two different definitions of low income: 'relative' low income (the current year median income) and 'fixed' or 'absolute' low income (the 1994/95 median income, adjusted for price inflation). Income is weekly disposable household income after housing costs, equivalised for household size and composition. The data source is Households Below Average Income, based on the Family Resources Survey (FRS).

The second graph measures those lacking a fridge/freezer, washing machine or telephone (the question intends to cover land-line telephones only). The data is split by the economic status of the highest income householder. The data is from the Scottish Household Survey, for 1999 and 2000 together.

Overall adequacy of the indicator: **high**. *The FRS is a well-established annual government survey, designed to be representative of the population of Great Britain as a whole. Note, however, that coverage does not extend beyond the Caledonian Canal. For the second indicator, the Scottish Household Survey is a large survey (including approximately 31,000 households over two years) designed to be representative of private households and of the adult population in private households in Scotland.*

Children and pensioners
with low income

The proportion of children and pensioners in low income households has not changed much since 1997/98.

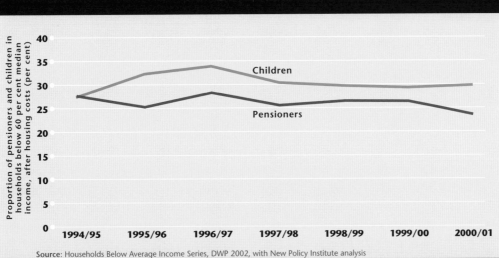

Source: Households Below Average Income Series, DWP 2002, with New Policy Institute analysis

Two-fifths of low income households with children are more than £50 a week short of the low income threshold.

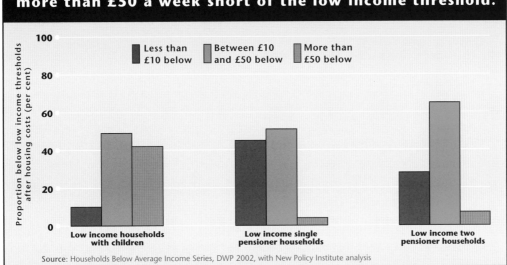

Source: Households Below Average Income Series, DWP 2002, with New Policy Institute analysis

The first graph shows the proportion of pensioners and children who are in low income households – defined as below 60 per cent of GB median income in the current year (see Indicator 1 for a more detailed definition).

The second graph measures the depth of low income. For each of the three groups (households with children, single pensioner households and two pensioner households) living in low income using the above definition, it shows the proportions of those in low income according to the amount by which they fall below the low income threshold (grouped into three bands: less than £10, £10–£50, and over £50 per week). Data is for 2000/01 and is not equivalised.

The data source for both graphs is Households Below Average Income, based on the Family Resources Survey (FRS) and analysis by the New Policy Institute.

*Overall adequacy of the indicator: **high**. The FRS is a well-established annual government survey. See Indicator 1 for more details. Adequacy of the second graph can be thought of as medium, as numbers below 60 per cent median are subject to greater uncertainty, particularly when looking at different family types separately.*

Income inequality

The proportion of people with incomes below any single low income threshold can only provide a partial picture of income poverty. As we have already seen [2b], some households still fall many tens of pounds a week short of the 60 per cent threshold, whilst others are only just short. How far people fall below the threshold (the *depth* of low income) is therefore as important to an understanding of income poverty as changes in the headline proportion (the *breadth* of low income). A fuller picture also requires information on the *duration* of low income, which measures the extent to which people on low income in one year are on it in the next or subsequent years. However, reliable data on this for Scotland does not yet exist.[11]

Another consequence of the way in which relative low income is now usually defined, in relation to *median* rather than *mean* income (that is, the income of the household at the very mid-point of the income distribution, rather than average household income), is that incomes in the upper half of the income distribution have no effect upon it. While this makes sense as far as *measuring* poverty is concerned, it may be insufficient for an *understanding* of it, as the same developments in society may be influencing both low income and high income.

Topics and indicators

The two indicators in this theme have been selected to provide a broader picture of the distribution of incomes in Scotland in recent years. The aspects addressed are:

▌ The income distribution around the relative low income threshold.

▌ High and low incomes in Scotland.

The income distribution in Scotland around the relative low income threshold is measured by three statistics together, showing **the proportion of people with incomes below 50 per cent, 60 per cent and 70 per cent of the British median household income in the current year** [3a]. The question with this indicator is whether, over time, the three statistics move together (implying that the breadth and depth of low income are changing in similar ways) or not.

The supporting graph [3b] shows **the proportions below the low income thresholds for different family types,** namely single adults with children, couples with children, other working age adults without children, and pensioners.

High and low incomes in Scotland are measured by two statistics, namely **the ratios of income at the 10th and 90th percentiles compared with median income** [4a]. The first of these measures income inequality in the lower half of the income distribution while the second measures income inequality in the upper half. The closer that these ratios are to 1, the lower is the degree of income inequality, and vice versa. The graph also shows the same ratios for England and Wales.

The supporting graph [4b] provides another inter-country comparison, showing Scotland's position in the 'European poverty league'. For this graph, unlike the others, the measure of median income used is the Scottish median rather than the British one, although for the particular measure used in this graph, there is virtually no difference between the two.

What the indicators show

▐ The proportion of the population below the 50 per cent and 70 per cent low income thresholds show the same slight upward trend over the four years to 2000/01 as the proportion below the headline (60 per cent) threshold. Both the breadth and depth of low income have therefore been moving in the same direction. [3a]

▐ Around two-thirds of lone-parent households fall below the 70 per cent low income threshold in 2000/01 (and more than half below the 60 per cent threshold), at least double the rate for any one else. [3b]

▐ Over the seven years to 2000/01, income inequality rose in Scotland, among both higher and lower incomes. In both cases, however, inequality is still less than in England and Wales (where it remained almost unchanged over the whole of the period). [4a]

▐ Comparing the three years after 1997/98 with the three years before, the rise in inequality in both the lower and upper halves of the income distribution in Scotland was about four per cent. Taken together, this means that the gap between the income of the household at the 90th percentile (the household one-tenth of the way down from the top of the income distribution) and the one at the 10th percentile (the household one-tenth of the way up from the bottom of the income distribution) rose by 8 per cent. [4a]

▐ On the latest available comparable data (for 1998), if Scotland appeared as a separate country within EU statistics, it would show a poverty rate similar to that of the UK as a whole, leaving it equal second behind only Greece in a European 'poverty league'. [4b]

Other key points and relevant research

▐ For Britain as a whole, a quarter of those on low income in 1996 were also on low income in each of the subsequent three years.[12]

Intensity of low income

Indicator
3

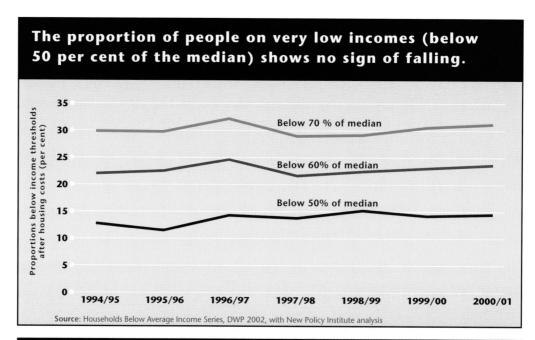

The proportion of people on very low incomes (below 50 per cent of the median) shows no sign of falling.

Source: Households Below Average Income Series, DWP 2002, with New Policy Institute analysis

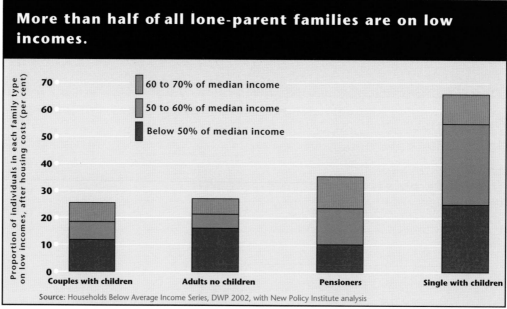

More than half of all lone-parent families are on low incomes.

Source: Households Below Average Income Series, DWP 2002, with New Policy Institute analysis

The first graph shows the number of people below 50 per cent, 60 per cent and 70 per cent of current year GB median income. The data is for years since 1994/95. See Indicator 1 for a more detailed definition.

The second graph, using data for 2000/01, shows the proportions below each of the three thresholds for each family type. The types are: one or more adults without children; couples with children; lone adults with children; and pensioners.

The data source for both graphs is Households Below Average Income, based on the Family Resources Survey (FRS) and analysis by the New Policy Institute.

*Overall adequacy of the indicator: **high**. The FRS is a well-established annual government survey. See Indicator 1 for more details. A qualification is that the numbers below 60 per cent are subject to greater uncertainty, particularly when looking at different family types separately due to lower sample sizes.*

Inequality in Scotland

Income inequality in Scotland has risen since the mid 1990s but is still less than in England and Wales.

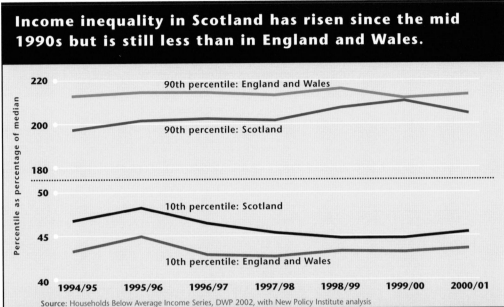

90th percentile: England and Wales

90th percentile: Scotland

10th percentile: Scotland

10th percentile: England and Wales

Source: Households Below Average Income Series, DWP 2002, with New Policy Institute analysis

Compared with other EU countries, Scotland and the rest of the UK ranked equally in 1998, with a higher proportion on relative low income than any other country except Greece.

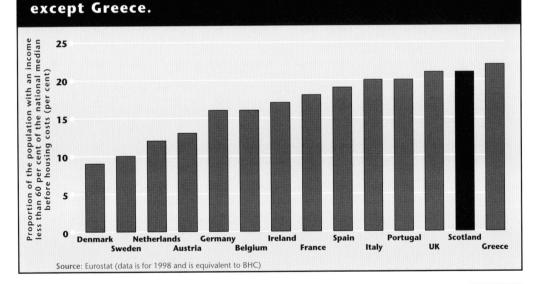

Source: Eurostat (data is for 1998 and is equivalent to BHC)

The first graph compares levels of income inequality since 1994/95 in the upper and lower halves of the income distribution using the ratios between income at the 90th percentile and median income, and income at the 10th percentile and the median. Figures are shown separately for Scotland, and for England and Wales, using the country-specific median. The measure of income is the same as for Indicator 1. The data source is Households Below Average Income, based on the Family Resources Survey (FRS) and analysis by the New Policy Institute.

The second graph shows the proportion of people in EU countries with an equivalised income that was less than 60 per cent of the median for their own country in 1998 on a before housing costs (BHC) basis. 60 per cent of median income is the preferred EU measure of levels of low income. The data source is the European Household Panel Survey. The figure for Scotland has been obtained by adjusting the UK proportion by the amount by which the proportion for Scotland below 60 per cent of the BHC median in the FRS is different from the corresponding proportion in FRS for Great Britain.

*Overall adequacy of the indicator: **high**. The FRS is a well-established annual government survey. See Indicator 1 for more details. For the second graph, note that data the European Community Household Panel is a smaller survey compared with the FRS and suffers from a loss of members over time. Adequacy of this graph can be regarded as medium.*

Geography: The pattern of low income

Where do people on low income in Scotland live? Someone answering that question on the basis of the stereotypical images presented would reply that the answer was first and foremost the Glasgow area, with parts of other large cities housing significant concentrations of low income residents too. Obviously, there is some truth to this: for example, using 1998 data, Glasgow City accounts for one-fifth of all claimants of Income Support and Jobseeker's Allowance, with North Lanarkshire, and the cities of Dundee and Edinburgh, accounting for a further fifth between them. Yet, even though this represents a significant concentration, it is still a minority. Even extending the group to include Inverclyde, Renfrewshire and West Dunbartonshire to the west of Glasgow, as well as Falkirk and West Lothian between Glasgow and Edinburgh, still only pushes this proportion just above half. Thus an image of low income that sees it overwhelmingly as a problem of the big cities and/or central Scotland is, at best, only partially correct.

Similarly, it is also important to recognise that low income is not a problem that is confined, overwhelmingly, to particular neighbourhoods, or small areas. Thus, while a quarter of those claiming Income Support or Jobseeker's Allowance in 1998 lived in just 10 per cent of Scotland's electoral wards, and two-fifths lived in just 20 per cent of wards, that still leaves the majority of people on low income living elsewhere.[13]

Topics, maps and indicators

The two maps and one indicator in this section pick up on two topics associated with the distribution of low income. They are:

▌ The pattern of low income across local authority areas.

▌ 'Pockets' of low income within local authorities.

Local data on low income is limited. National surveys cannot provide reliable data at ward level: indeed, the official low income data (used for Indicators 1 to 4) is not now released even at the local authority level. We are therefore obliged to rely on administrative data on social security benefits and, increasingly, on tax credits, which is routinely available at local authority level and, with much of a delay, at ward level too. Although low income is more extensive than dependence on benefit, administrative data on benefits is the best proxy available.

Map A shows the distribution of low income across local authorities of wards with a high proportion of people claiming various means-tested benefits. It is based on **a count of the number of wards in each local authority with high proportions of claimants of either Income Support, Jobseeker's Allowance or Family Credit**. A ward is defined as being 'high' where the proportion of adults claiming one of these benefits is 25 per cent or above. Just under 1 in every 10 wards is 'high' on this definition. This map uses a colour coding whereby the darkest colour is reserved for the two authorities with ten or more high wards; the next darkest colour shows those with four or five high wards; the next, those with two or three high wards; and the last, those with one high ward. Those with no high wards are left uncoloured.

The pattern of low income across local authority areas is represented on the second map and a supporting graph [5b] which show **the proportion of the adult population in receipt of a key, social security benefit.**[14] Since this data does not include the Working Families Tax Credit, this indicator pertains to adults who are not working. This map introduces the colour scheme used most often for the maps in this volume: the darkest shade showing the 'worst' (i.e. highest) four, the next darkest showing the next four, the third darkest showing the next eight and the remaining sixteen left blank.

The other graph for this indicator [5a] shows how **the proportion of all those in Scotland claiming a key benefit who live in one of the four local authorities with the highest rates of claim** – namely Glasgow City, North Lanarkshire, Inverclyde and West Dunbartonshire – has changed over time. Figures are shown separately for claimants of working age and for pensioners. The pensioner data, however, has only been made available for the last three years. This graph is one measure of the extent to which claimants are becoming more or less concentrated in particular local authority areas.

What the maps and indicators show

▌ Of the 92 wards in Scotland in 1999 with 'high' numbers of people on low income, Glasgow had 44, followed by Dundee with 10. The next local authority areas were North Lanarkshire (5), Inverclyde (4) and Edinburgh City (4). Glasgow, and indeed Dundee, therefore stand out. [Map A]

▌ Map A also shows that 21 of Scotland's 32 local authority areas had at least one such ward with a high rate of low income. As well as Western Isles (3) and Fife (2), they include a number with low rates of low income for the local authority area as a whole, namely Dumfries and Galloway (2), Scottish Borders, Highland, Aberdeen City and East Dunbartonshire (1 each).

▌ The four local authorities with the highest average rates of people on low income [5b and Map B] in 2001/02, as measured by the proportion of the adult population claiming a key benefit, are Glasgow City (34 per cent), North Lanarkshire and Inverclyde (both 29 per cent) and West Dunbartonshire (28 per cent).

▌ Between them, these four local authorities (with 22 per cent of the total adult population) account for 33 per cent of the total number of working age claimants of key benefits and 28 per cent of pensioner claimants [5a]. Pensioner claimants are therefore somewhat less geographically concentrated than working age claimants. These proportions have been falling over recent years, but only very slightly. Concentration at the local authority level, therefore, has really not changed.

▌ Fifteen of the 32 Scottish local authority areas have more than 1 in 5 of their adults claiming a key benefit [5b]. Even in the authority with the lowest rate of claim (Aberdeenshire), more than 1 in 8 of all adults are claiming a key benefit. While the problem of low income is indeed most extensive in the big cities, especially Glasgow and some of its surrounding districts, there are substantial numbers of people suffering from it in all parts of Scotland, including sparsely populated, rural ones.

Other key points and relevant research

∎ Forty-two of the 50 most deprived postcode sectors in the 1998 Scottish Area Deprivation Index had Glasgow codes, the other 8 being 3 each from Edinburgh and Dundee and 1 each from Motherwell and Paisley.[15]

∎ The figures quoted in the opening remarks above – to the effect that just over a quarter (27 per cent) of those claiming Income Support or Jobseeker's Allowance in 1998 lived in just 10 per cent of Scotland's electoral wards, while just over two-fifths (44 per cent) lived in just 20 per cent of wards – imply a somewhat lower level of concentration in Scotland than in England. In England, the comparable figures are that a third of all claimants live in the top 10 per cent of wards with the highest claim rates, while over half live in the top 20 per cent.[16]

MAP A: Although more than half the small areas with high levels of dependence upon means-tested benefits are in Glasgow and Dundee, 21 local authorities have at least one such area.

LAs with 10 or more high wards
LAs with 4 or 5 high wards
LAs with 2 or 3 high wards
LAs with 1 high ward
LAs with no high wards

Enlarged section of the central belt (indicated on map by orange border)

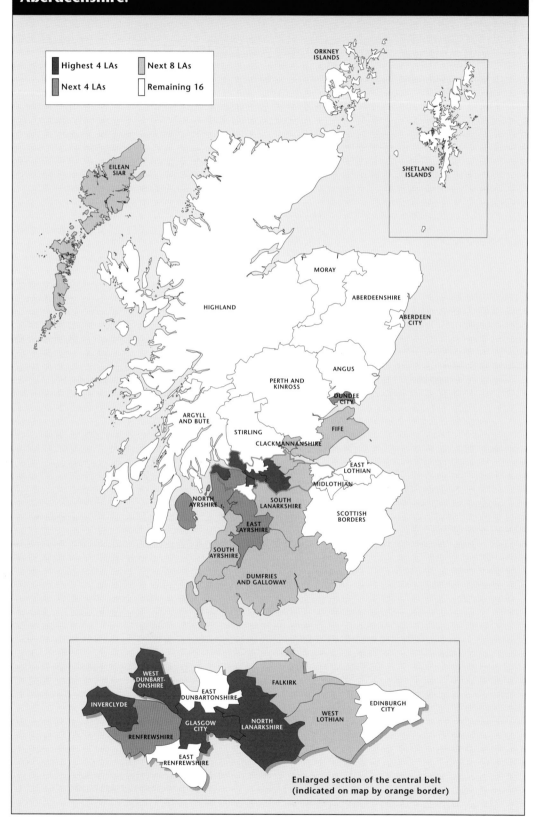

MAP B: The proportion of adults receiving one or more of the key benefits ranges from one in three in Glasgow to one in seven in Aberdeenshire.

Highest 4 LAs   Next 8 LAs

Next 4 LAs   Remaining 16

Enlarged section of the central belt
(indicated on map by orange border)

Spread of low income

The proportion of those claiming one or more of the key benefits who live in the four authorities with the highest rate of claim has barely fallen over recent years.

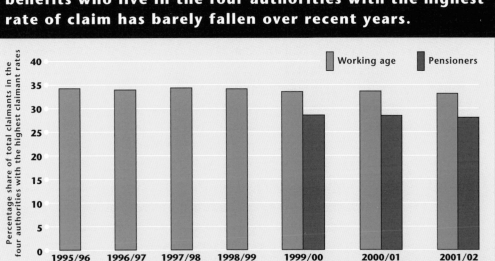

Source: Client Group Analysis, Quarterly Bulletin on Population of Working Age, DWP 2002.

The proportion of adults receiving one or more of the key benefits ranges from 1 in 3 in Glasgow to 1 in 7 in Aberdeenshire.

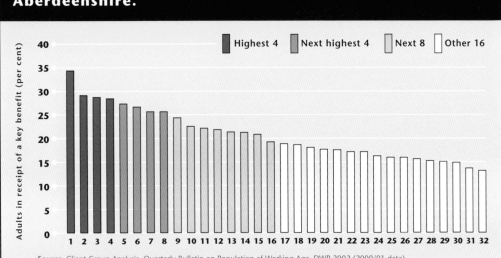

Source: Client Group Analysis, Quarterly Bulletin on Population of Working Age, DWP 2002 (2000/01 data)

The first graph shows the proportion of those claiming at least one key benefit in the four local authorities with the highest proportion of the population making a claim. They are: Glasgow City, North Lanarkshire, Inverclyde and West Dunbartonshire. The data is split to show claimants of working age (from 1995/96) and those of pensionable age (from 1999/00) separately. These represent the earliest years for which the data is available. 2001/02 is the latest year for which data is available.

The second graph accompanies the map and shows the distribution of local authorities according to the proportion of their adult populations who are in receipt of a key benefit. The data is for 2001/02.

Key benefits are: Income Support (IS), Jobseeker's Allowance (JSA), Incapacity Benefit (IB), Severe Disablement Allowance (SDA) and Disability Living Allowance (DLA).

The data source for both graphs is the DWP Information Centre.

Overall adequacy of the indicator: **high**. *The data is thought to be very reliable. It is based on information collected by the DWP for the administration of benefits.*

Benefit dependency among working age people

Interpreting the number of people who are dependent on social security benefits requires more care now than it did before the benefit reforms that have taken place since 1997. In particular, both the value of some benefits and the number of people who are made better off by them have greatly increased. The two benefits for which this is particularly true are the pensioners' entitlement to Income Support (re-labelled as the Pensioner Minimum Income Guarantee) and Family Credit (converted into the Working Families Tax Credit, or WFTC) for working families with children. As a result, receipt of these benefits and credits is no longer necessarily a sign of very low income, and neither is an increase in the number of people receiving them necessarily a bad thing.

On the other hand, the improvements in benefit levels have not been universal: whereas those in work with children and pensioners may have gained, those of working age who are not working have not, particularly if they have no dependent children. As the value of benefits for this latter group have risen only in line with inflation, their situation has been steadily worsening relative to the average (median) household, by around 10 per cent over five years.

Topics and indicators

In order to avoid ambiguities of interpretation as far as possible, the indicators selected under this heading exclude the means-tested benefits (and the successor tax credits) that are available to people in work. They also exclude Child Benefit. The two aspects of benefit dependency addressed are:

▌ The number of working age claimants of key benefits.

▌ The number of long-term, working age claimants of these benefits.

The **number of working age claimants of key benefits** is represented by Indicator 6a, divided between those claiming means-tested benefits (reflecting low income) and those claiming other benefits. It should be noted that this excludes the predecessor to WFTC, namely Family Credit. A decline in the numbers here over time is to be recognised as an improvement.

The supporting graph for this indicator [6b] shows the amount of money per week by which those who are entirely dependent on Income Support or Jobseeker's Allowance, fell short of the 60 per cent relative low income threshold in autumn 2000. Figures are presented for a variety of different types of family and assume that housing costs are met entirely by Housing and Council Tax Benefit. The figures therefore represent the amount of money left over to pay for everything else.[17]

Indicator 7a, **the number of long-term working age claimants of non-work benefits**, is defined exactly as the previous indicator, except that it is restricted to people of working age who have been claiming a benefit continuously for two years or more.

Once again, the interpretation here is clearly that a reduction in these numbers would represent an improvement.

The supporting graph [7b] shows the composition of this group according to the reason why they are in receipt of benefit.

What the indicators show

▐ Since 1997, there has been a much smaller fall in the number of long-term working age claimants of these 'key' benefits (down 17,000 or 5 per cent) than in the total number of working age claimants (down 70,000 or 11 per cent). [6a and 7a]

▐ Among long-term claimants, four-fifths are sick or disabled. The majority of the remainder are lone parents. [7b]

▐ There is great variation in the amount of money by which households on means-tested benefits fall short of the relative low income threshold. So while the figure for single pensioners was around £10 a week at the end of 2000, it was almost £50 a week for single adults under 25. The figure was around £27 a week for lone parents, compared with £70 for working age couples. [6b]

Other key points and relevant research

▐ Although broadly similar, the fall in the number of working age claimants in Scotland over the last five or so years has been slightly smaller than in England (but almost identical to Wales): 12^1/$_2$ per cent over the period February 1997 to February 2002 compared with 15 per cent.[18]

▐ The number of people on a means-tested benefit fell more slowly in Scotland between 1995 and 2001 than in Great Britain as a whole (a reduction of 15 per cent compared with 25 per cent).[19]

▐ The reduction in the number of people of working age in long-term receipt of a key benefit since 1999 is similar in Scotland as in Great Britain as a whole – a fall of 5 per cent.[20]

Working age people in receipt of benefit

Indicator
6

The number of people of working age receiving both means-tested and contributory benefits continues to fall gradually.

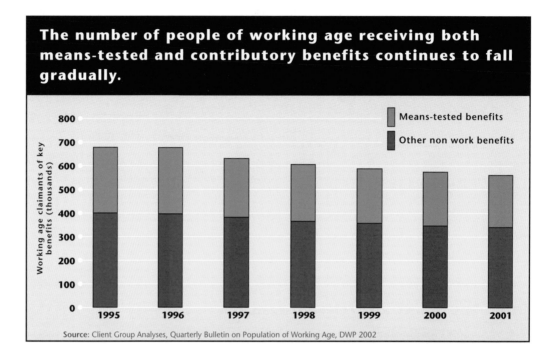

Source: Client Group Analyses, Quarterly Bulletin on Population of Working Age, DWP 2002

In 2000, working age couples solely reliant on Income Support were between £65 and £75 a week below the low income threshold.

Source: Households Below Average Income Series, DWP 2000–01; Income Support data, DWP Information Centre (ASD) 2002 and NPI calculations

The first graph shows the total number of working age people in receipt of one or more key benefit. The data is split to show those in receipt of a means tested benefit (IS and JSA) and those in receipt of other benefits (IB, contribution-based JSA, SDA and DLA) separately. See Indicator 5 for full names of benefits. The data source is the DWP Information Centre.

The second graph measures the difference in pounds per week between benefit levels in December 2000 for recipients of all ages of Income Support (or income-based Jobseeker's Allowance, or for pensioners on the Minimum Income Guarantee) split by family type and the low income threshold of 60 per cent of median income. A value of £3.58 per child per week for free welfare foods (for children under school age) and free school meals has been added in to the income. This is based on a weighted average of DWP equivalent figures. The figures assume that the household lives in rented accommodation, with rent and council tax fully covered by the corresponding benefits. Data is not equivalised.

The data is from the Family Resources Survey (FRS) and Income Support data from the DWP Information Centre.

*Overall adequacy of the indicator: **high**. The data is thought to be very reliable and provides an accurate count of those on benefit, whilst the FRS is a reliable annual government survey.*

Long-term receipt of benefits

The number of people of working age receiving a key benefit for two years or more has not changed much since 1997.

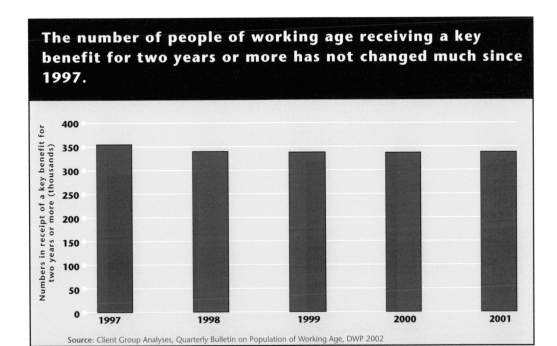

Source: Client Group Analyses, Quarterly Bulletin on Population of Working Age, DWP 2002

The vast majority of working age long-term recipients of a key benefit are sick or disabled.

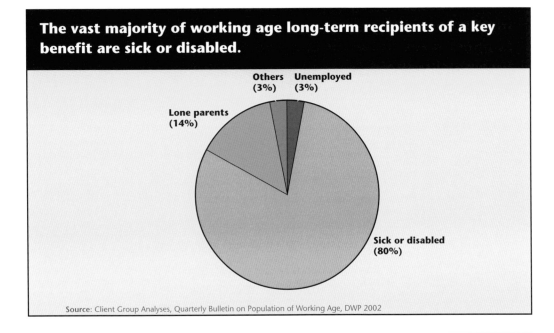

Source: Client Group Analyses, Quarterly Bulletin on Population of Working Age, DWP 2002

The first graph shows all those of working age who were in receipt of a key benefit for two years or more (key benefits being IS, JSA, IB, SDA or DLA). It is therefore based on the same definition as graph 6a except that it measures long-term recipients – a subset of the previous graph. Data is for August of each year for years since 1997 – the earliest year that this data is available.

The second graph breaks down the data for the latest year by type of claimants: unemployed, sick and disabled, lone parents and others (e.g. carers, asylum seekers).

The data source for both graphs is the DWP Information Centre.

Overall adequacy of the indicator: **high**. *The data is thought to be very reliable. It is based on information collected by the DWP for the administration of benefits.*

Commentary

Addressing income poverty through the private sector

Jim McCormick, Research Director, Scottish Council Foundation

It is a common assumption that reducing poverty is beyond the powers of both local government and the Scottish Executive, and of little interest to the private sector.[21] This view deserves to be challenged. By seeking to improve local conditions for private services, government at every level can play a vital gatekeeping function, improving access to affordable services and helping to develop sustainable opportunities for private services where markets are currently weakest.

Using the different policy instruments at their disposal, Westminster and Holyrood can combine to tackle income poverty in better ways. As the UK government seeks to reduce poverty through the minimum wage, tax credits and welfare benefits, the Scottish Executive can address the issue from another direction by coordinating action by the private sector to reduce the costs that low-income households face.

Research evidence shows that the lowest income households are disproportionately affected by market as well as by public service failures. Not only do they have less money coming into the house, they face higher costs going out. Consumer benefits arising from competition have largely failed to reach low income communities: poverty is coupled with restricted choice. Some of the specific issues that low income households face include:

▌ Higher costs for water, home energy and telephone services for those unable to use direct debit as a means of payment.

▌ Higher domestic fuel bills as a result of inefficient heating systems, poorly insulated houses, etc.

▌ Higher costs for credit and cheque cashing due to limited access to credit unions or other appropriate financial services (e.g. banks willing to make small loans at low rates of interest).

▌ Low/no returns on small savings as a result of interest rate structures on savings accounts.

▌ Higher costs for home and car insurance as a result both of the characteristics of the local area and of inappropriate products (e.g. too high a minimum insurable value).

▌ Higher costs for food and other basic goods because of lack of physical access to larger, cheaper shops.

Through a combination of regulation, private sector engagement with the inclusion agenda and local anti-poverty action, wider access to cheaper and higher quality services can be stimulated. This approach is, however, much more likely to succeed when public agencies, including social housing authorities, act as gatekeepers between the private sector and low income households, pooling their combined purchasing power to create lower cost and more viable market opportunities than exist on a household-by-household basis.

By way of an example, such an approach has been applied, somewhat unevenly, to the problem of financial exclusion. Financial exclusion is usually the result of a number of factors rather than simply refusal by banks and insurance companies to serve customers on a low income. Standard bank accounts, with their potential for unexpected charges and loss of control are viewed as unsuitable by many people. The withdrawal of bank branches from poor urban neighbourhoods and remote and rural communities has restricted the availability of products. A recent study of insurance cover found that most low-income households are excluded because the cost of premiums or strict security improvements is too high.

Ideally, the way to measure the extent to which low income – and other disadvantaged – groups face higher costs for basic goods and services would be to have a comprehensive 'cost of living' index for each group which could then be compared with the indices for other groups. In practice, however, this is an ambitious undertaking as well as one that is bound to provoke intense dispute about innumerable matters of detail. Simpler alternatives, any one of which touches on a particular aspect of the problem, are therefore needed. Three kinds of measure are required:

▮ First, measures of the difference in cost for what is basically the same product. For example: gas or electricity according to how it is paid for; insurance premiums according to the locality; and perhaps a simple basket of essential goods according to the locality and type of shop. These measures should include perceptions of value for money offered by providers.

▮ Second, measures of how far various disadvantaged groups – especially those on low income but also those in rented accommodation, the sick and disabled, lone parents and ethnic minorities – possess certain basic goods and services, ranging from bank accounts to central heating.

▮ Third, measures of the extent to which private sector suppliers are working with intermediary organisations, especially housing associations but also trade unions, workplace cooperatives and community organisations, to ensure that their products and services are available to low income and other disadvantaged groups. Evidence of how basic products are being promoted, and measures of take-up, will also be required to ensure tailoring of products is based on demand-side considerations. The extent to which households feel they have a genuine choice between providers might also be tracked, to focus attention on the uneven spread of competitive rather than monopoly supply.

While some of the data needed to create these measures exists already, much of it does not – and in any case, what is most important is that the Scottish Executive itself should deem these things to be important. With greater commitment from both the Executive and local government and a clearer challenge to private service providers, more comprehensive cost-cutting packages could be applied to household energy bills, food, transport and other financial services. If a combined reduction of 20 per cent can be achieved on basic household bills in low income communities (as suggested by the Community Development Foundation), this would have a substantial impact on the well-being of many of the poorest people in Scotland.

Summary

All individuals with low income

The proportion of people in households with relative low incomes has been rising gently since 1997/98. In contrast, the proportion below a fixed income threshold has been falling. Around a fifth of all households where the highest income householder is not in work lack a washing machine, a fridge or a telephone.

Children and pensioners with low income

The proportion of children and pensioners with low income households has not changed much since 1997/98. Two-fifths of the households with children on low income are more than £50 a week short of the low income threshold.

Intensity of low income

The proportion of people on very low incomes (below 50 per cent of the median) shows no sign of falling. More than half of all lone-parent families are on low incomes.

Inequality in Scotland

Income inequality in Scotland has risen since the mid-1990s but is still less than in England and Wales. Measured against the EU low income threshold, Scotland and the rest of the UK ranked equally in 1998, with a higher proportion on relative low income than any other country except Greece.

Spread of low income

The proportion of those claiming one or more of the key benefits who live in the four local authorities with the highest rate of claim has barely fallen over recent years. The proportion of adults receiving one or more of the key benefits ranges from 1 in 3 in Glasgow to 1 in 7 in Aberdeenshire.

Working age people in receipt of benefit

The number of people of working age receiving both means-tested and contributory benefits continues to fall gently. In 2000, working age couples solely reliant on Income Support were between £65 and £75 a week below the low income threshold.

Long-term receipt of benefits

The number of people of working age receiving a key benefit for two years or more has not changed much since 1997. The vast majority of people of working age who are long-term recipients of a key benefit are sick or disabled.

Chapter 2 Employment and education

Theme	Indicator/map
Employment and education risk factors for poverty	Indicator 8: Risk of low income Indicator 9: Risk of unemployment
Education performance	Indicator 10: Low attainment at school Indicator 11: Qualifications of school leavers Indicator 12: Destination of school leavers
Unemployment and economic inactivity	Indicator 13: Economic status of those of working age Indicator 14: Households without work for two years or more
Geography: employment patterns	Map C: In receipt of Working Families Tax Credit Indicator 15: In receipt of Working Families Tax Credit Map D: Blue-collar employment Indicator 16: Blue-collar employment
Disadvantage at work	Indicator 17: Low pay and pay inequalities Indicator 18: Insecure at work Indicator 19: Without access to training

Employment and education risk factors for poverty

Since 1997, the UK government has promoted a twin strategy for helping people out of poverty: 'work for those who can' and 'education for all' – not just for children and young adults but as lifelong learning for all those of working age.

Despite the importance that has been attached to these two ideas, however, it has never been wholly clear what they actually mean in practice. For example, how much paid work do households have to do before they can expect to have escaped from low income? Does almost any extra qualification help reduce the risk of poverty, or are some qualifications much more important than others?

With no powers over the social security system or employment law, the Scottish Executive has limited scope to depart from the approach to employment laid down by Westminster. The levels of low income, which are determined by the tax and benefit system, the minimum wage and regulations on workers' entitlements, are therefore largely a reflection both of UK priorities and of UK policies.[1] In education, by contrast, within its overall strategy of promoting lifelong learning, the Scottish Executive acts independently with a range of initiatives of its own.[2]

Topics and indicators

Using Scottish evidence, the indicators in this section shed light on two aspects of the many connections between education, employment and low income. They are:

▌ The risk of low income according to the household's economic status.

▌ The risk of unemployment according to the individual's level of education.

The risk of low income in Scotland is examined by an indicator [8a], showing the **probability of working age households having an income below the relative low income threshold according to their economic status.**[3] Households are grouped into four types: *all working* (single adult households where the adult is working full-time and two adult households with one working full-time and the other working at least part-time); *some working* (other working households); *unemployed*; and *other* (including lone-parents and sick and disabled). There are two points of interest: the difference in the risks between one group and another; and any change in the risks since 1994/95.

The supporting graph [8b] shows the **share that each of the four household types represents among low income households**, with figures presented for two sets of three years, namely 1994/95 to 1996/97 (the last three years of the Conservative government) and 1998/99 to 2000/01 (the three most recent years for which data is available).

The risk of unemployment according to the individual's level of education in Scotland is represented by an indicator [9a], which shows the **probability of being unemployed according to the individual's highest level of qualification.** The link between educational status and unemployment is less direct and therefore less easy to interpret than that between a household's economic status and its income.

The supporting graph [9b] provides a slightly different view of the same subject, focusing on **the unemployment rates for those aged under 25** with men and women shown separately. In order to show the risk for the corresponding age group as a whole, the rates are expressed as a percentage of the total male or female population at that age.

What the indicators show

▌ The risk of falling below the relative low income threshold varies hugely according to a household's economic status, between almost 75 per cent for the unemployed and 5 per cent for fully working households. In households where no one has more than part-time work or where one person is working full time and one not at all, the risk of low income is around 20 per cent. [8a]

▌ Although the risk of low income is much lower among working households than non-working ones, working households still accounted for 40 per cent of all low income households in the years 1998/99 to 2000/01 (as there are many more such households). [8b]

▌ Despite the fact that there has been little change in the overall proportion of low income households in Scotland since the mid-1990s, there have been some marked changes in their economic status, with those who are unemployed falling from 25 to 19 per cent and those who are fully employed rising from 6 to 9 per cent. [8b]

▌ This last figure highlights the fact that, though small in absolute terms, the risk of low income among fully working households rose from an average of $2^3/4$ per cent over the period 1994/95 to 1996/97 to $4^1/4$ per cent over the period 1998/99 to 2000/01. [8a]

▌ There is an almost four-fold variation in the risk of unemployment among those counted as economically active depending on their level of education: from around $3^1/2$ per cent among those with a higher education qualification, to around $13^1/2$ per cent with no qualification. Those whose highest qualification is a Standard Grade or equivalent face a 10 per cent chance of being unemployed, apparently irrespective of whether the grades they achieved were high or not. [9a]

▌ Around 12 per cent of men in Scotland aged between 16 and 24 are unemployed, which is almost twice the rate for men aged over 25. The rate among women aged 16 to 17 is similar – although the percentage falls back more rapidly with age, with the all-average rate applying even to women in their early 20s. [9b]

Other key points and relevant research

▌ Another risk factor for unemployment is ethnicity. For example, research finds the unemployment rate among minority ethnic women to be double that of white women.[4]

▌ The importance of qualifications is increasing, with a greater proportion of jobs requiring a broader range and higher level of skill than ever. In 1997, sixty-nine per cent of jobs in the UK required at least basic qualifications, compared with 62 per cent in the mid-1980s.[5]

Risk of low income

**The risk of low income varies greatly, depending on
whether a household has paid work, and how much it
has. These risks have risen slightly, even for working
households, over recent years.**

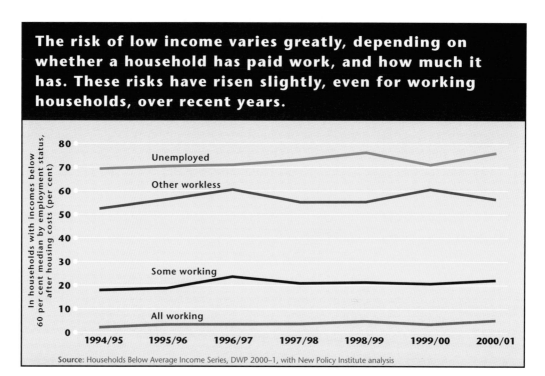

Source: Households Below Average Income Series, DWP 2000–1, with New Policy Institute analysis

**Among those in low income households, the proportion who are
unemployed has fallen while the proportion who are working
has risen.**

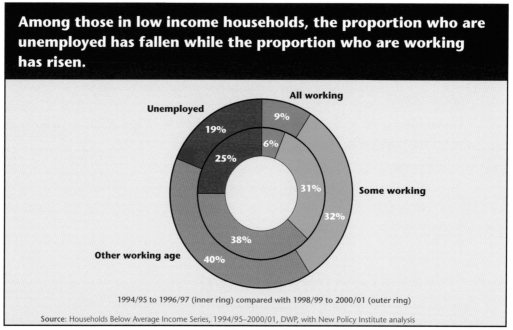

1994/95 to 1996/97 (inner ring) compared with 1998/99 to 2000/01 (outer ring)

Source: Households Below Average Income Series, 1994/95–2000/01, DWP, with New Policy Institute analysis

The first graph shows the proportion of working age people in each economic status category who are in households with incomes below 60 per cent of the median, measured after housing costs (see Indicator 1 for a more detailed definition). 'All working' comprises single or couples, all in full-time work; plus those couples where one is in full-time and one in part-time work. 'Some working' comprises the self-employed; plus one in full-time work, one not working; plus no one full-time but one or more in part-time work. 'Unemployed' comprises households where there is no one in paid work and where the head of the household or spouse is unemployed. 'Other' comprises those that are economically inactive and workless (primarily the sick and disabled and lone parents). The data is for years since 1994/95.

The second graph shows the proportion of those of working age in low income households by the same four 'economic status' categories, and compares changes in these statistics between 1994/95 to 1996/97 and 1998/99 to 2000/01.

The data source for both graphs is Households Below Average Income, based on the Family Resources Survey (FRS) and analysis by the New Policy Institute.

*Overall adequacy of the indicator: **high**. The FRS is a well-established annual government survey (see Indicator 1 for more details).*

Risk of unemployment

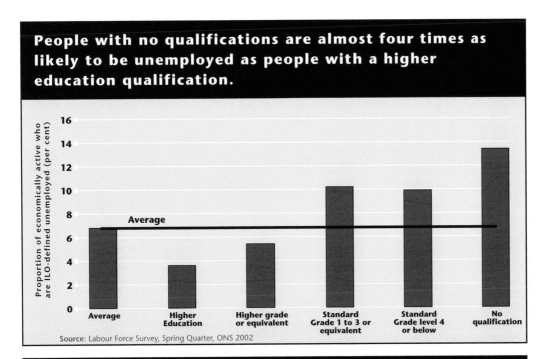

People with no qualifications are almost four times as likely to be unemployed as people with a higher education qualification.

Source: Labour Force Survey, Spring Quarter, ONS 2002

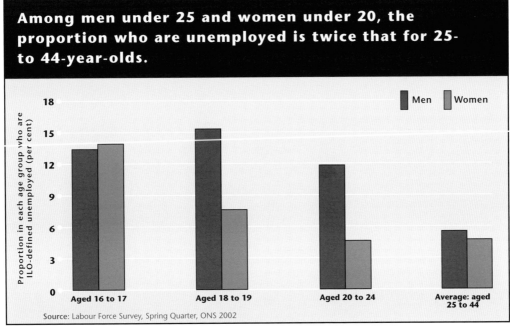

Among men under 25 and women under 20, the proportion who are unemployed is twice that for 25- to 44-year-olds.

Source: Labour Force Survey, Spring Quarter, ONS 2002

The first graph looks at the proportion of the economically active working age population who are ILO-defined unemployed by their highest educational qualification. As there are many possible qualifications, these have been grouped into a limited number of groups after taking advice from both the Scottish Executive and the Department for Education and Skills. Those who have a highest qualification which is not classifiable in the Labour Force survey (around 5 per cent of the total) have not been shown on the graph on the grounds that they are likely to be a very disparate group.

The second graph shows the ILO-defined unemployment for the same year for the following age groups, shown separately: 16–17, 18–19, 20–24 and 25–44.

Data for both graphs is from the Labour Force Survey with analysis by the New Policy Institute.

*Overall adequacy of the indicator: **high**. The LFS is a well-established, quarterly government survey of 60,000 households, designed to be representative of the population as a whole.*

Education performance

In this section, we look at how well the Scottish education system is serving pupils in terms of both the qualifications they acquire at the age of 16 and their immediate prospects on leaving school. An independent report in 1998 expressed concern that the needs of the lowest qualified fifth of pupils within Scotland were not as well served as they might be, with progress among this group being less than progress for the average pupil, resulting in a widening gap between those with fewest qualifications and the rest.[6]

This concern with the fortunes of the bottom fifth of pupils has been explicitly picked up by the Scottish Executive, one of whose Social Justice 'Milestones' is to bring 'the poorest-performing 20 per cent of pupils (in terms of Standard Grade achievement) closer to the performance of all pupils'.

With high rates of unemployment still prevalent among young adults, especially men right through to their mid-20s, it is also necessary to focus on what happens to people in the years immediately after school. The destination of school leavers, and the level of qualifications they have acquired by the end of their teens, are important markers towards future prospects, especially in view of the fact that training delivered through work goes disproportionately to those who already possess qualifications.

Topics and indicators

This section addresses the following three topics:

▮ Educational performance of the least qualified pupils.

▮ Qualification levels of those leaving school with no more than Standard Grades.

▮ The destination of school leavers.

Educational performance of the least qualified pupils has to be looked at both in terms of how that performance itself is changing and how it compares with the change in the average performance of all pupils. It is therefore represented by an indicator showing **the standard level tariff scores of the weakest performing 20 per cent of pupils compared to the average** [10a].[7] Tariff scores are calculated by converting the levels that 16-year-olds achieve in their Standard Grade exams into points, with the points ranging from 38 for a Standard Grade 1 (roughly equivalent to a GCSE 'A' in England and Wales) to 11 for a Standard Grade 5 (the first 'low grade') and 3 for a Standard Grade 7 (the lowest result). Progress is being made on this indicator when the score for the lowest fifth is rising faster than the score for the average.

The supporting graph for this indicator [10b] shows **the proportion of 19-year-olds without basic qualifications**. Those with nothing more than a Standard Grade 7 and with nothing more than an SVQ2 or equivalent are shown separately.

The qualification level for those leaving school with no more than Standard Grades [11a] provides a more detailed look at educational performance for the over half of pupils who do not go on to obtain Highers. This is a larger proportion of the population than this report is usually concerned with, but such concern is justified by the relatively high risk of unemployment (around 10 per cent according to Indicator 9a) faced by those with no more than Standard Grades. The indicator is **the proportion of school leavers by their highest grade** over time, with the results broken down into no grades, low grades, middle grades and high grades.[8] This also provides insight into why the average tariff scores are changing as they are.

The supporting graph [11b] shows the breakdown of those with no or low grades (defined here as a Standard Grade 4 or below) according to their father's social class.

The destination of school leavers is represented by an indicator [12a] which shows **the proportion going into full-time higher or further education, training and employment**, with a residual category of 'other'. The main focus of interest in this graph is on this 'other' category, where a reduction would represent progress on the grounds that education, training or work are the 'desirable' destinations.

The supporting graph [12b] draws on the same source to show, for the most recent year, how the proportion going to the different destinations varies between local authorities.

What the indicators show

▌ As measured by the 'tariff score', exam results for both the lowest fifth of pupils and pupils on average rose steadily between 1995 and 2001, by 13 and 19 points respectively. This is equivalent to a one grade improvement in two exams for the lowest fifth and three exams on average. The gap between the lowest fifth of pupils and the average is therefore widening, albeit by a relatively small amount. [10a]

▌ In 2002, 6 per cent of 19-year-olds had no qualifications, and a further 16 per cent had no qualification higher than an SVQ2 (or equivalent). Both proportions are now back to 1996 levels, after haven risen and then fallen in the years in between. [10b]

▌ The results by the highest level of qualification achieved show that, after falling between 1996/97 and 1998/99, the proportion of school leavers gaining either no or low Standard Grades has remained static, with around 6 per cent gaining nothing and a further 3 per cent gaining nothing higher than a Standard Grade 5. [11a]

▌ By contrast, the proportion gaining Standard Grades at the highest level has risen quickly and steadily, from 16 per cent in 1996/97 to 24 per cent in 2000/01. This has not, however, had any effect on the proportion for whom Standard Grades are their highest achievement, which has remained steady at around 55 per cent over the five years. [11a]

▌ The breakdown of these results by social class shows the percentage of pupils from manual backgrounds obtaining either low qualifications or none at all to be around four times the percentage for those from non-manual backgrounds. [11b]

▌ The last decade has witnessed a big rise in the proportion of school leavers going into either full-time higher or further education, up from two-fifths a decade ago to one-half now. It has also witnessed a big fall in the proportion going into non-employment based training. The proportion not going into education, training or work has, however, remained unchanged over the decade, at around 1 in 6. [12a]

▌ There are considerable differences between local authorities in the proportion of school leavers going to different destinations (education, training and work). The largest such range is for full-time higher education (from 20 per cent for Glasgow City to 53 per cent for East Renfrewshire). Glasgow City also has the highest proportion (28 per cent) going to destinations other than education, training or work. [12b]

Other key points and relevant research

▌ Concerns about performance at the lower end of the educational spectrum is highlighted by Scotland's relatively high level of illiteracy compared with other developed countries. In 1997, OECD research suggested that around 20 per cent of people in Scotland are at the lowest literacy level and that a further 30 per cent might find their skills inadequate to meet the demands of a 'knowledge society'.[9]

▌ Research suggests that the inequality in educational outcomes between social classes is worsened by the concentration of pupils from lower socio-economic classes in particular schools.[10]

▌ Research into the level of attainment on entry to Primary 1 in Aberdeen in 1999 found that levels of literacy and numeracy were already notably lower amongst pupils from areas of multiple deprivation and that progress in literacy over the course of the first year was similarly less marked among pupils from disadvantaged backgrounds.[11]

▌ Although rates are not directly comparable, the proportion of 19-year-olds without any Standard Grades at Level 6 or above in Scotland (6 per cent) is slightly lower than the proportion not achieving any GCSEs at Grade G or above in England and Wales (8 per cent).[12]

Low attainment at school

Indicator
10

Standard grade attainment both for pupils on average and pupils in the bottom 20 per cent has risen since 1995, but the gap between them remains wide.

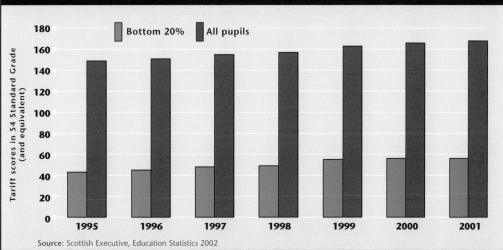

Source: Scottish Executive, Education Statistics 2002

The proportion of 19-year-olds with either no or low qualifications is now back at the levels of six years ago, after having risen and then fallen in the years in between.

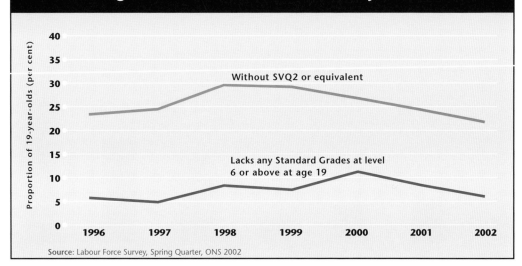

Source: Labour Force Survey, Spring Quarter, ONS 2002

The first graph shows tariff scores at S4 of the lowest performing 20 per cent of pupils and scores for all pupils separately. The data is for years since 1995 – the earliest available. The data is from the Scottish Executive.

Tariff scores are calculated by converting each grade achieved at S4 (including Standard Grades and vocational qualifications) into a score. Higher grades receive higher scores and vice versa. The graph shows the average tariff score for the 20 per cent of pupils with the poorest qualifications, and the average tariff score for all pupils (which includes the former category).

The second graph shows the proportion of 19-year-olds who lack a SVQ2 or equivalent, with those lacking any Standard Grades (no passes at Level 6 or above) shown separately. SVQ2 or equivalent includes those with 5 or more Standard Grades Credit level (Standard Grades 1–2); GNVQ intermediate; RSA diploma; City and Guilds craft; BTEC, SCOTVEC first or general diploma; A levels or five or more O Levels/GCSEs grade A–C.

The data source is spring quarters of the Labour Force Survey.

Overall adequacy of the indicator: **high**. *Qualifications data is collected by the Scottish Executive Education Department and is based on data from all schools. Data for the second graph is based on survey data.*

Qualifications of school leavers

Indicator
11

After falling between 1996 and 1998, the proportion of school leavers gaining no or low Standard Grades has remained static. There has been a big rise in the proportion leaving school with high Standard Grades.

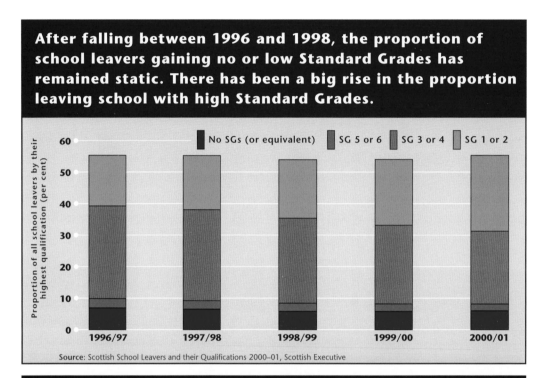

Source: Scottish School Leavers and their Qualifications 2000–01, Scottish Executive

Pupils whose fathers are from manual backgrounds are more likely to get poor scores at Standard Grade than other pupils.

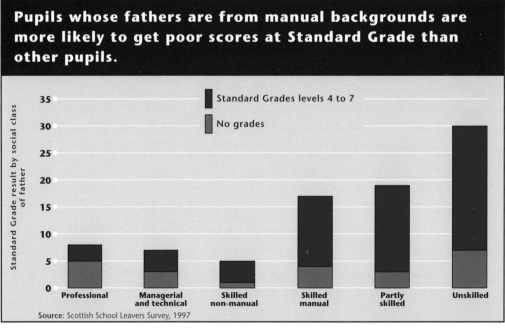

Source: Scottish School Leavers Survey, 1997

The first graph show the proportion of school leavers whose highest qualification was a Standard Grade, by the highest grade attained. The data shows those with: no Standard Grades (SGs); with SG 5 or 6; with SG 3 or 4 and with SG 1 or 2. The data is from 1996/97 to 2000/01, the earliest and latest year respectively for which data is available. The data is School Leavers data from the Scottish Executive.

The second graph shows pupils achieving no grades or low grades at Standard Grade in S4 (final year of compulsory schooling). Low grades are defined as Standard Grade levels 4 to 7 only. The data is according to the social class of the pupils' fathers and relates to all school leavers in 1997. It is from the Scottish School Leavers Survey 1997 (the latest available).

*Overall adequacy of the indicator: **high**. Data for the first graph is based on administrative data on attainment of all school leavers and is reliable. Data for the second graph is taken from a survey that is designed to be representative.*

Destination of school leavers

Indicator
12

Over the last decade, while the proportion of school leavers entering higher of further education has risen steadily, the proportion entering training has more than halved.

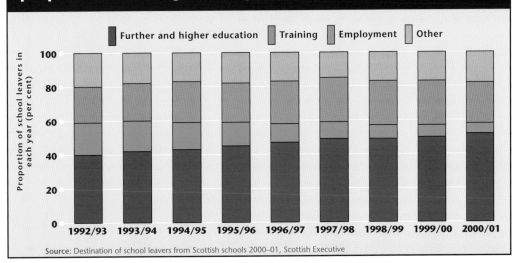

Source: Destination of school leavers from Scottish schools 2000–01, Scottish Executive

There are big variations between local authorities in the proportion of school leavers going into education, into training and into work.

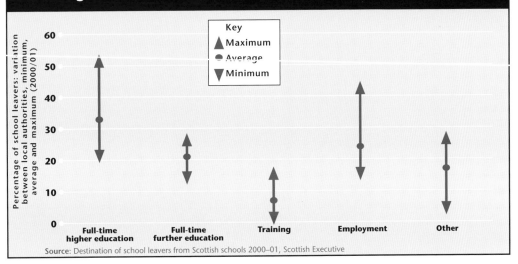

Source: Destination of school leavers from Scottish schools 2000–01, Scottish Executive

The first graph shows the destinations of school leavers. Of all school leavers in each year it shows separately the proportions entering further and higher education, training and employment. The 'other' category includes school leavers going into none of these: who are known by the education authority or school to be unemployed, sick, at home looking after children or caring for the elderly, involved in full-time unpaid voluntary work, or taking time out. In addition it also includes all leavers whose destinations are not recorded by the careers service, independent or grant-aided schools.

The second graph shows data for 2000/01. It shows the variations between local authorities in the proportions of school leavers' going to different destinations. It shows the rates for the local authorities with the highest and lowest proportion of school leavers for each category, as well as the average.

Data for both graphs is the Destination of Leavers from Scottish Schools: 2000/01, published by the Scottish Executive.

Overall adequacy of the indicator: **high**. *The indicator is derived from administrative data collected by the Scottish Executive. Information on publicly funded schools is provided to the Scottish Executive by the careers services. Information from independent schools is collected directly from the schools.*

Unemployment and economic inactivity

Indicator 8a has shown how workless working age households face a very high risk of low income. This is obviously true for those households officially counted as unemployed, where one or more adults are both seeking and available for work. But it is equally true for that far larger number of households where the adults are deemed to be economically inactive, due chiefly either to being sick or disabled, or because the adult is a lone parent. The trend in the number of these households is therefore going to be a major factor in whether poverty is rising or falling.

Among those deemed economically inactive, a substantial minority report that they would take paid work if it were available. Although there are many reasons why people would fall into this category, it is important to pay attention to this group, who occupy an intermediate position between the tightly and administratively defined 'unemployed' and the much larger and varied 'economically inactive'.

Finally, while some households at least will be able to endure short periods of worklessness without suffering too much, it is incontestable that those without work for years who are reliant solely on state benefits are bound to find themselves in straitened circumstances. Among working age households, the long-term workless are at the core of the problem of poverty.

Topics and indicators

The indicators here, which are for working age households only, relate to:

▌ Trends in work and worklessness.

▌ Households without work in the long term.

In addition, the supporting graphs pick out some important angles on these matters, namely variations in worklessness by age and sex and the uneven relationship across Scotland between unemployment and economic inactivity.

Trends in work and worklessness are captured by an indicator that shows **the proportion of the working age population who are either unemployed or economically inactive** [13a]. The interpretation of this graph is straightforward, although it is important to look for falls in both measures, rather than just unemployment alone. It also implicitly shows the trend in the proportion who are employed.

The supporting graph [13b] shows **the proportion unemployed alongside the proportion who are economically inactive but report that they want work**, with figures shown separately for men and women and for three different age groups.

Households without work in the long term is illustrated by Indicator 14a, which shows **the number of households without work for two years or more**, with the small minority who have been workless for between two and three years shown separately. Again, the interpretation of this graph is straightforward.

The supporting graph [14b] presents a breakdown of **the relationship between rates of male and female unemployment and rates of male and female economic inactivity** (measured, as before, as a share of all men and women aged 25 to retirement). Results, which are broken down by age, are shown for the 32 Scottish local authorities gathered into four equal groups, according to the rate of male ILO-defined unemployment prevailing in each.

What the indicators show

- Although the proportion who are unemployed has been declining steadily for much of the last decade, the proportion who are economically inactive has only been coming down consistently since 1999. As a result, employment in early 2001 was higher than it had been for a decade (2.3 million people, or 73 per cent of the working age population) – although by 2002 employment had fallen back slightly. [13a]

- On average, some 4 per cent of men and women aged between 25 and 64 (men) and 20 and 59 (women) are officially unemployed, while some 7 per cent are economically inactive but wanting work. Official unemployment may therefore capture little more than one-third of the true extent of what could be called 'involuntary worklessness'.

- While the proportion of both men and women who are officially unemployed declines with age, the proportion who are economically inactive but wanting work rises for men as they get older, with the rate twice as high for men aged 55 to 64 as that for men aged 25 to 54. By contrast, these rates are highest among women in their 30s. [13b]

- Rates of economic inactivity *for both men and women* are on average higher in areas where official unemployment among men is higher. So in the eight local authority areas with the highest rates of male unemployment, a further 22 per cent of men and 31 per cent of women are economically inactive. By contrast, in the eight authorities with the lowest male unemployment rates, a further 10 per cent of men and 22 per cent of women are economically inactive. [14b]

- In 2002, the number of working age households who had been workless for two years or more was the same as the previous peak, in 1995. At more than 200,000, the number who had been workless for three years or more was at its highest for at least a decade. [14a]

Other key points and relevant research

- The largest part of 'disguised unemployment' is among those classified as sick and disabled. The UK has the highest rate of working age sickness in the EU, despite the fact that it does not have the highest rate on a range of health indicators.[13]

- In 1997, researchers calculated that, including a proportion of 'discouraged workers', people on sickness benefits, government schemes and those who had taken early retirement, the 'real rate' of unemployment for Glasgow City was 31 per cent compared to the official claimant count rate of 12 per cent.[14]

- The number of households without work for three years or more has shown similar trends over time in Scotland as in the UK as a whole – both have increased even though unemployment has fallen.

Economic status of those of working age

Indicator
13

The proportion of the working age population who are unemployed has been falling for at least a decade. The proportion who are economically inactive has been falling only since 1999.

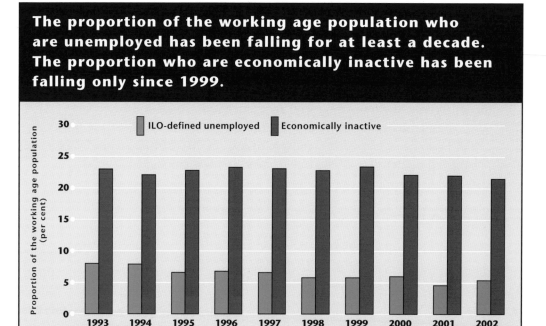

Source: Labour Force Survey, Spring Quarter, ONS 2002

While the proportion of men and women who are unemployed falls with age, the proportion of men who are economically inactive but would like work rises with age.

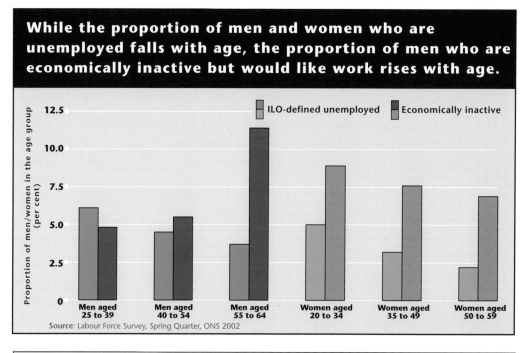

Source: Labour Force Survey, Spring Quarter, ONS 2002

The first graph shows separately the proportion of people of working age who are unemployed (on the ILO definition) as well as those counted as 'economically inactive'. This latter group includes people of working age who do not have work and are not seeking work; those who do not have work but would like work and are not available to start work for some time and those not actively seeking work.

The second graph shows data for the spring quarter of 2002 for those who are ILO-defined unemployed and those who are counted as economically inactive who want work (shown separately). Note that this differs from the first graph which is broader and includes all who are inactive rather only those who want work. The data is split by age group and sex.

Data for both graphs is from the Spring Quarter of the Labour Force Survey (LFS) with analysis by the New Policy Institute.

Overall adequacy of the indicator: **high**. *The LFS is a well-established, quarterly government survey of 60,000 households, designed to be representative of the population as a whole.*

Households without work
for two years or more

Indicator
14

**In 2002, more than 200,000 households had been
workless for three years or more, the highest number
in the past decade.**

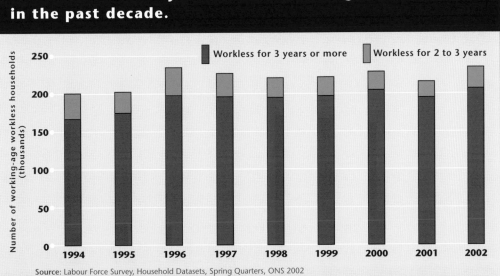

Source: Labour Force Survey, Household Datasets, Spring Quarters, ONS 2002

**Rates of economic inactivity among both men and women
are higher in areas where the proportion of men who are
unemployed is higher.**

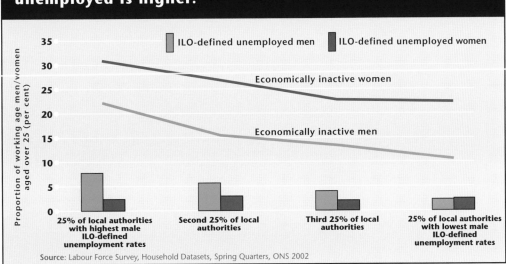

Source: Labour Force Survey, Household Datasets, Spring Quarters, ONS 2002

The first graph shows the total number of working age households where no-one has worked for two years or more. The upper part of the bar shows how many have been workless for between two and three years. The lower part shows how many have been workless for three years or more.

The second graph compares the distribution of economic inactivity and ILO-defined unemployment rates for men and women aged 25 to retirement age (shown separately) for the spring quarter of 2002. It divides local authorities into quarters according to the level of male ILO-defined unemployment, showing those with the highest 25 per cent through to those with the lowest 25 per cent.

Data for both graphs is from the Labour Force Survey (LFS) Household datasets for the spring quarter of each year. Data for the second graph includes analysis by the New Policy Institute.

Overall adequacy of the indicator: **high**. *The LFS is a well-established, quarterly government survey of 60,000 households designed to be representative of the population as a whole.*

Geography: Employment patterns

The focus on the geography of employment in this section reflects a view among researchers that the problems of unemployment and worklessness in Scotland cannot be fully understood without reference to the kinds of jobs that are available in particular localities.[15]

The immediate background to this is that during the mid and late 1990s, when the total number of jobs was either steady, or even rising, the number of blue-collar jobs was continuing to fall. The deeper background to this is the wholesale loss of jobs in Dundee, Glasgow, Clydeside and the former coal fields over the past quarter century, Glasgow for example having lost two-thirds of its manufacturing jobs between 1972 and 1996.[16] If, as has been argued, upward mobility from manual jobs is low, especially among men,[17] the loss of so many blue-collar jobs can only have very serious consequences.

Concern about the availability of jobs carries over into the effectiveness of the single most important policy that the UK government has introduced to try to encourage people into work, namely the Working Families Tax Credit (WFTC). The question here is how well the WFTC is benefiting more deprived areas in terms of its effects upon employment, the concern being that in such areas it is the limited demand for labour that is really holding down employment.[18]

Topics, maps and indicators

This section picks up these concerns via the topics of:

- In-work benefits and tax credits.

- Blue-collar employment.

In-work benefits and tax credits are illustrated in Map C, which shows the **claimant rate for WFTC by local authority area** for 2001/02. The rate of claim is expressed as the number of claims as a percentage of women of working age. The supporting graph [15b] shows the spread of values of these rates across local authorities.

The principal graph in this pair [15a] shows **the annual claimant rates for WFTC and its predecessor, Family Credit, for four groups of local authority areas from 1995/96.** The groupings have been built up according to each authority's rate of benefit dependency among adults of working age who are not working.

Interpretation of this indicator is not straightforward. Unlike the number of working age people in receipt of out-of-work benefits, tax credits, which are linked with work, are viewed favourably. Indeed, they have been designed so that many more people are eligible for them than for Family Credit, and people are encouraged to claim them. Reflecting this viewpoint, a rise in rates over time [15a] is interpreted as an improvement, while Map C and supporting indicator 15b draw attention to both high-claim and low-claim areas.

Patterns of employment are illustrated in Map D, which shows **the percentage change between 1995 and 2000 in jobs in industry, agriculture (including fishing and forestry), and transport by local authority area** with the supporting graph [16b] showing the range of figures for the 32 authorities. The data is drawn from business surveys[19] and refers to the jobs available within the area, rather than the jobs performed by the people who live there. The particular grouping of jobs has been selected as being broadly reflective of manual work.

The other graph associated with this map [16a] shows the **change in the total number of jobs in Scotland over the period from 1999 to 2002**, with jobs divided into three groups: industry and agriculture (including forestry and fishing); public sector services; and private sector services (including transport).

What the maps and indicators show

❚ The proportion claiming WFTC varies across Scotland from around 5 per cent in East Dunbartonshire, Edinburgh and Aberdeenshire, to above 10 per cent in Dundee, East Ayrshire and the Scottish Borders. [Map C and 15b]

❚ Claims for WFTC across Scotland as a whole have been rising since its introduction in October 1999, from 5½ per cent in 1999/2000 to 8 per cent in 2001/02. There was also a small but steady rise in the numbers claiming its predecessor, Family Credit, at least in the period 1995/96. [15a]

❚ Although claims for WFTC are highest in more deprived areas, the size of the rise since 1999/2000 is about the same irrespective of the underlying level of deprivation, at around three percentage points. [15a]

❚ Against a background of almost no change in the total number of jobs in industry, agriculture and transport over the period, Scottish Borders, West Dunbartonshire, Edinburgh and the Ayrshires recorded falls of more than 10 per cent in this category of jobs over the period 1995 to 2000. Rises in excess of 30 per cent were seen in Aberdeenshire, Angus, Perthshire and Kinross and West Lothian. [16b and Map D]

❚ In terms of the total number of jobs in Scotland, the period 1999 to 2002 saw a sharp change in the mix, with industrial and agricultural jobs falling by 66,000 (down 12 per cent) while both public and private sector service jobs rose in number, by 78,000 and 56,000 respectively (up 12 and 6 per cent). [16a]

Other key points and relevant research

❚ The last three years of declining blue-collar employment alongside growing white-collar employment in Glasgow continues a trend from earlier years; thus, between 1993 and 1998, Glasgow lost nearly 5,000 jobs in manufacturing and construction while gaining 4,800 in distribution, 16,200 in banking and financial services and 10,100 in public administration.[20]

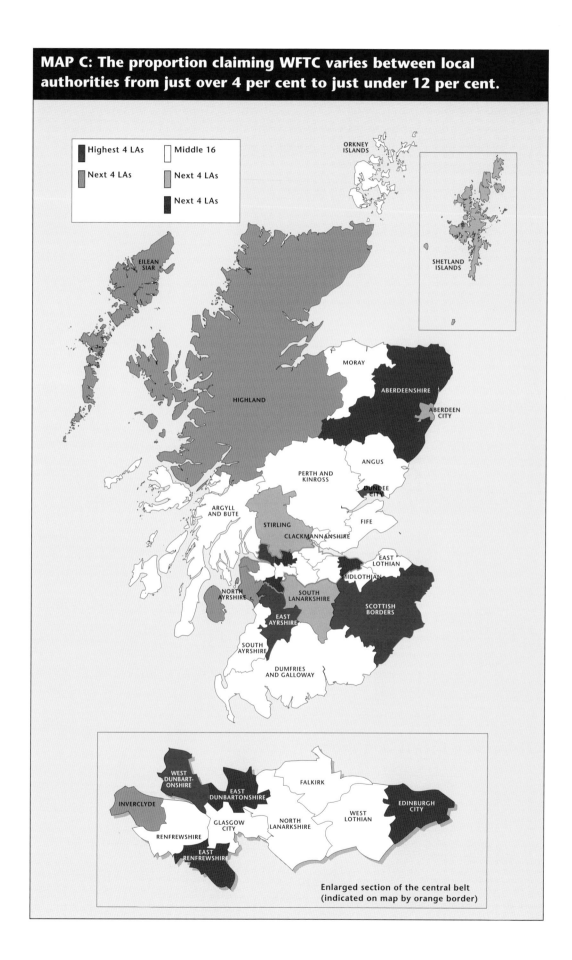

MAP C: The proportion claiming WFTC varies between local authorities from just over 4 per cent to just under 12 per cent.

Highest 4 LAs   Middle 16
Next 4 LAs   Next 4 LAs
                  Next 4 LAs

ORKNEY ISLANDS

SHETLAND ISLANDS

EILEAN SIAR

HIGHLAND

MORAY

ABERDEENSHIRE

ABERDEEN CITY

ANGUS

PERTH AND KINROSS

DUNDEE CITY

ARGYLL AND BUTE

FIFE

STIRLING

CLACKMANNANSHIRE

EAST LOTHIAN

MIDLOTHIAN

NORTH AYRSHIRE

SOUTH LANARKSHIRE

SCOTTISH BORDERS

EAST AYRSHIRE

SOUTH AYRSHIRE

DUMFRIES AND GALLOWAY

WEST DUNBART-ONSHIRE

EAST DUNBARTONSHIRE

FALKIRK

INVERCLYDE

EDINBURGH CITY

GLASGOW CITY

NORTH LANARKSHIRE

WEST LOTHIAN

RENFREWSHIRE

EAST RENFREWSHIRE

Enlarged section of the central belt
(indicated on map by orange border)

In receipt of Working Families Tax Credit

Indicator
15

The introduction of Working Families Tax Credit (WFTC) has benefited all areas more or less equally, with about 3 per cent more people of working age claiming WFTC than claimed its predecessor, Family Credit.

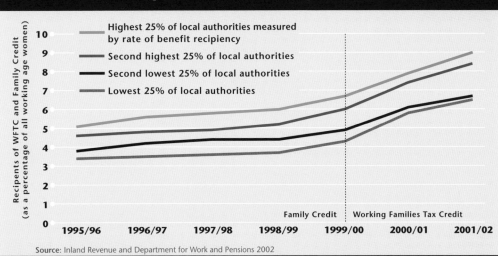

Source: Inland Revenue and Department for Work and Pensions 2002

The proportion claiming WFTC varies between local authorities from just over 4 per cent to just under 12 per cent.

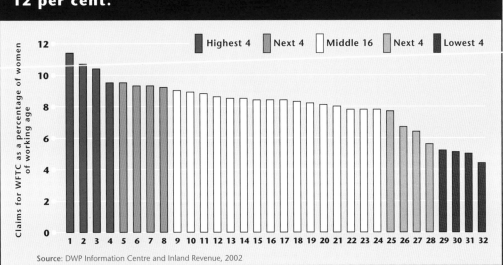

Source: DWP Information Centre and Inland Revenue, 2002

The first graph shows the proportion of people in receipt of Family Credit and its replacement in October 1999, the Working Families Tax Credit (WFTC), as a proportion of all women of working age. The data is split by local authorities which are grouped into quarters according to their rates of recipiency showing those with the highest through to the lowest rates. Data is for 1995/96 to 2001/02 – the earliest and latest dates for which the data was available.

The second graph accompanies the map and shows the distribution of WFTC recipiency by local authority. The graph measures the number of claims for WFTC as a proportion of population of women of working age. The data is split by local authority, which are grouped into fours: the four local authorities with the highest WFTC claim rate, the next four, the middle sixteen, the next four and the four with the lowest rate. The data is for 2001/02.

The data source is the Department for Work and Pensions Information Centre for data on Family Credit, Inland Revenue for data on WFTC and New Policy Institute analysis.

*Overall adequacy of the indicator: **high**. The data is thought to be very reliable and provides an accurate count of those on benefit/tax credits.*

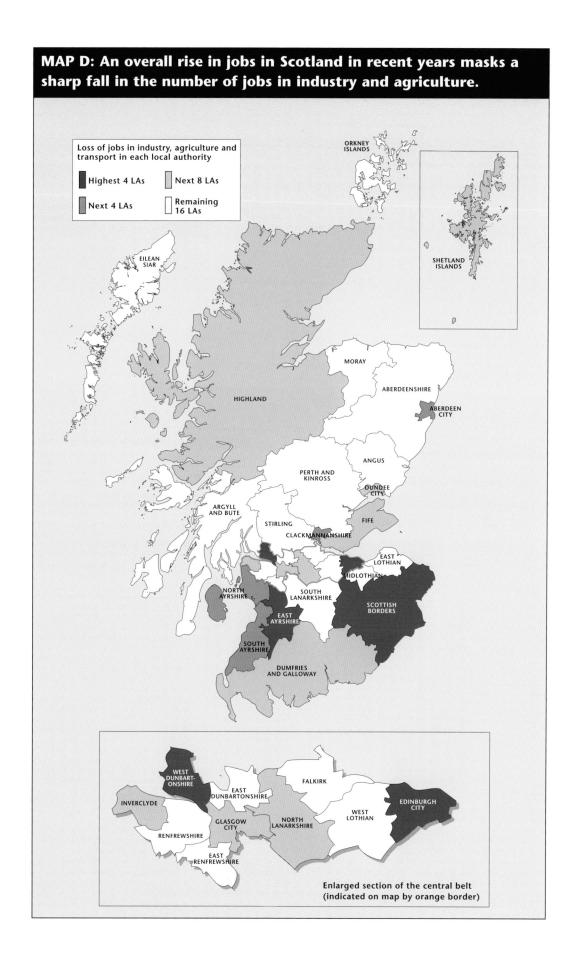

MAP D: An overall rise in jobs in Scotland in recent years masks a sharp fall in the number of jobs in industry and agriculture.

Loss of jobs in industry, agriculture and transport in each local authority

- Highest 4 LAs
- Next 4 LAs
- Next 8 LAs
- Remaining 16 LAs

Enlarged section of the central belt (indicated on map by orange border)

Blue-collar employment

Indicator
16

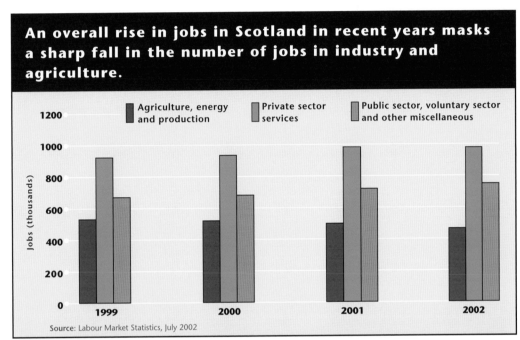

An overall rise in jobs in Scotland in recent years masks a sharp fall in the number of jobs in industry and agriculture.

■ Agriculture, energy and production ■ Private sector services ■ Public sector, voluntary sector and other miscellaneous

Jobs (thousands)

1999 2000 2001 2002

Source: Labour Market Statistics, July 2002

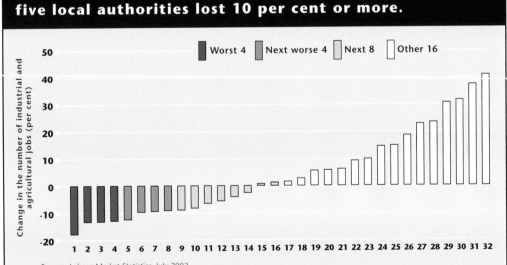

While the total number of jobs in industry, agriculture and transport changed little between 1995 and 2000, five local authorities lost 10 per cent or more.

■ Worst 4 ■ Next worse 4 □ Next 8 □ Other 16

Change in the number of industrial and agricultural jobs (per cent)

1 2 3 4 5 6 7 8 9 10 11 12 13 14 15 16 17 18 19 20 21 22 23 24 25 26 27 28 29 30 31 32

Source: Labour Market Statistics, July 2002

The first graph shows the number of jobs split by industry showing (separately) agriculture, energy and production, private sector services and public and voluntary sectors. 'Agriculture, energy and production' includes agriculture, forestry, fishing, mining, energy and water, manufacturing and construction.

Data is yearly data from Labour Market Statistics, Scotland and is based on the Labour Force Survey (LFS).

The second graph accompanies the map and shows how the proportion of jobs in the industrial, agricultural and transport sectors have changed between 1995 and 2000 in each local authority. The data is arranged to show the four local authorities with the largest loss in these jobs, the next four, the next eight and remaining half.

Data is yearly and taken from the Local Authority Economic Briefing from the Scottish Executive. Estimates of employee jobs are taken from the 2000 Annual Business Inquiry (ABI), and Annual Employment Survey (AES) results for 1995, scaled to be consistent with the ABI. The employee jobs figures are taken from the NOMIS database, and due to confidentiality constraints, exclude employee jobs in agriculture.

*Overall adequacy of the indicator: **high.** The LFS is a well-established, quarterly government survey of 60,000 households designed to be representative of the population as a whole. Data for the second graph can be regarded as limited. Whilst the LFS component of this data is robust, data derived from the ABI and AES are subject to sampling error, with information for areas based on relatively small samples. Therefore figures should be treated with some caution.*

Disadvantage at work

Although raising the level of employment is central to the UK government's anti-poverty strategy, work does not always guarantee an escape from poverty, especially for those households where the adults are less than fully employed. The conditions of employment and pay of some workers mean that they may be only marginally better off than people without work and so still fall below the official poverty line. In fact, except for lone parents, the minimum wage (and any entitlements to the Working Families Tax Credit) is not sufficient to remove any but fully working households from poverty.[21]

Furthermore, since employment rates in Scotland are at a recent high, reductions in poverty in the future will require an improvement in the quality of employment, especially of low paid jobs. Besides the rate of pay, this includes the duration of employment, pay for sickness and holiday, pension arrangements and training. For Britain as a whole, the people most likely to receive formal training at work are those who are already better qualified.[22] As a result, disadvantage that originates in poor outcomes during school years is perpetuated during working age.

Topics and indicators

The indicators in this section address three specific subjects. They are:

▌ Low pay.

▌ Insecure forms of work.

▌ Training at work.

The leading candidate for an indicator on *low pay* would be one that measured the number of people earning rates of pay both around and above the minimum wage. Remarkably, however, the preferred official source of data on low pay has been declared unreliable for these purposes by the Office for National Statistics, at least for Scotland, while the source of data on pay that is considered reliable is believed to under-represent those in low paid work.[23]

Instead, therefore, our indicator [17a] focuses on pay differentials, measured by **the ratios of gross pay at the 90th percentile, and gross pay at the 10th percentile, to the median gross pay** – in other words, the pay of people one-tenth of the way from the top and bottom of the pay distribution respectively, each compared with the pay of the person in the middle. The latter ratio is a fair measure of how those on low pay are faring relative to the average, while the former provides information to allow comparison between differentials in the upper and lower halves of the pay distribution. The figures are shown separately for men and women.

The supporting graph [17b] shows **the variations in gross hourly earnings for manual workers for 2001 by industry group**, with separate figures for men and women.

'Insecure forms of work' is concerned with the problem of people who find themselves

taking a succession of jobs interspersed with periods of unemployment. The indicator selected here [18a] is **the proportion of people making a new claim for Jobseeker's Allowance who were last claiming less than six months ago.** A fall in this proportion would represent an improvement.

It is supported by a graph [18b] showing the **principal reasons people give for taking part-time or temporary work.** In each case, the main point of interest is those taking these forms of work who would prefer, respectively, full-time work or permanent work.

Training at work is concerned with whether work-based training is a benefit that is enjoyed at least as much by those with low levels of qualification as others. Indicator 19a shows the **proportion of people who have had some work-based training in the last three months, for those with some previous qualifications and those without.** As usual with this kind of graph, the interest lies both in the trend for those with low qualifications, and their position relative to others.

The supporting graph [19b] provides further detail, showing the **proportions receiving training in the most recent year according to their particular level of qualification.**

What the indicators show

▌ The inequality of gross earnings for both men and women widened slightly over the past decade, in both the lower and upper half of the earnings distribution. [17a]

▌ Gross hourly rates of pay for manual work for men vary substantially by industry, ranging from £5.67 in hotels and restaurants and £5.97 in agriculture, hunting, forestry and fishing, through to £8.68 an hour in manufacturing and £10.02 in energy and water. [17b]

▌ Depending on the industry, average hourly rates of pay for manual work are between 17 per cent and 28 per cent lower for women than for men. [17b]

▌ The proportion of those people making a claim for Jobseeker's Allowance (JSA) who last made a claim less than six months ago rose from 37 per cent in 1992 to 46 per cent in 2002. [18a]

▌ While some two-thirds of part-time employees report that they do not want full-time employment, only about a quarter of temporary employees report that they do not want permanent work. While a sole reliance on part-time employment is therefore associated with higher risks of low income [18a] part-time employment is for many a positive choice. [18b]

▌ Around a third of people in employment with educational qualifications received some job-related training over a three month period, compared with a tenth of those with no educational qualifications. Both proportions have been on a rising trend since at least 1994, but the differential between them has remained unchanged. [19a]

▌ These differentials exist, too, among those with qualifications: for example, those with higher educational qualifications are more than 1½ times as likely to receive training as someone with no more than higher grade or equivalent. [19b]

Other key points and relevant research

▮ Low pay is a particular issue in rural Scotland, where the tourist industry, agriculture and related activities – low paid sectors and often seasonal – are significant employment sectors.[24]

▮ A notable aspect of the labour market experience of people from ethnic minorities is their concentration in a limited range of industries. According to a 1991 survey conducted by the Scottish Office, 45 per cent of minority ethnic men were employed in distribution, catering, hotels and repairs – traditionally low paid sectors – compared with only 11 per cent of white men.[25]

▮ Research shows a significant correlation between job insecurity, 'poor general health' and tension in family relationships. It also suggests that people do not adjust well to job insecurity, with physical and mental well-being continuing to deteriorate the longer employees remain in a state of insecurity.[26]

▮ Median male earnings in Scotland are $2^{1}/_{2}$ per cent less than in Great Britain as a whole, with female median earnings being 5 per cent less.

▮ Earnings inequalities for men are now somewhat less in Scotland than in Great Britain as a whole, after being similar 10 years ago. For women, both the levels of inequality and the trends over time are similar in Scotland and in Great Britain as a whole.

▮ In the 1990s, temporary, part-time and self-employed jobs, as well as employment requiring a lower level of skill than their previous occupation, were the main ways in which unemployed people re-entered the labour market – 75 per cent of those re-entering took such jobs.[27]

▮ In only a minority of cases does part-time employment lead to better or more permanent employment. Under 25 per cent of those taking part-time employment in 1990–92 had full-time employment by 1995. Sixty-one per cent of those who had taken temporary contracts either remained on temporary contracts or were again unemployed.[28]

▮ Since reaching a peak in 1997, the number of people in Scotland on part-time contracts has fallen back by a fifth, to around 130,000 in 2002.[29]

▮ The proportion of people making a new claim for JSA who were claiming less than six months ago is similar in Scotland and in Great Britain as a whole.[30]

▮ A similar proportion of those without qualifications received job-related training in Scotland and in Great Britain as a whole, but the trend over time has been less favourable (no change in Scotland compared with gentle improvement in Great Britain as a whole).[31]

Low pay and pay inequalities

Indicator 17

Earnings have become more unequal over the past decade, for both men and women.

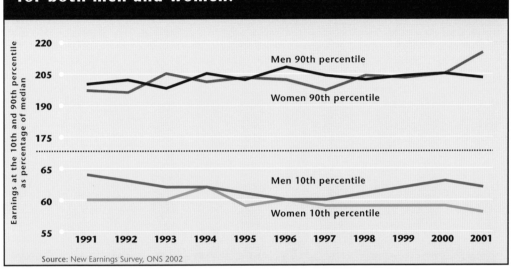

Source: New Earnings Survey, ONS 2002

Depending on the industry, average hourly rates of pay for manual work are between 17 per cent and 28 per cent lower for women than for men.

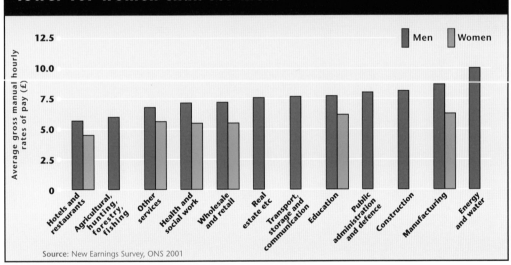

Source: New Earnings Survey, ONS 2001

The first graph shows earnings for men and women shown separately at the top and bottom of the income distribution, expressed as a percentage of the median. The left-hand axis shows the level of earnings at the 10th percentile (the lowest paid 10 per cent) and the right-hand axis shows the level of earnings at the 90th percentile (the highest paid 10 per cent).

The second graph shows average gross hourly rates of pay for manual workers for 2001. Data is split by sex (where data available) and industry type. Note that data on women in manual work is not available for all industry types.

Data for both graphs is taken from the New Earnings Survey (NES).

*Overall adequacy of the indicator: **high**. The NES is an annual survey of employers and is based on a 1 per cent sample of all employees based on records held by the Inland Revenue. Note that the NES does not include data on employees who are not members of the PAYE income tax schemes and is therefore likely to underestimate levels of earnings at the very bottom of the pay scale, especially in the informal economy.*

Insecure at work

Just under half the people making a new claim for Jobseeker's Allowance were last claiming less than six months ago.

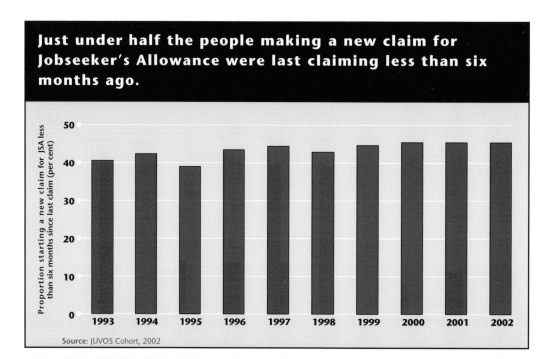

Source: JUVOS Cohort, 2002

Only 1 in 10 part-time employees want a full-time job – but 4 in 10 temporary employees would like a permanent job.

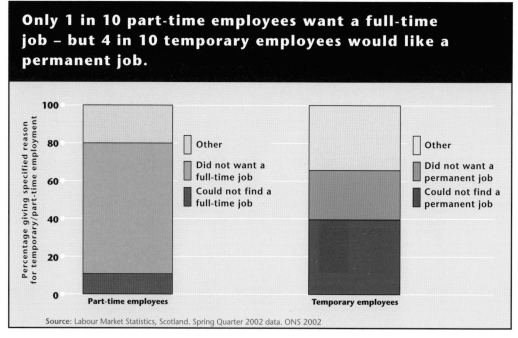

Source: Labour Market Statistics, Scotland. Spring Quarter 2002 data. ONS 2002

The first graph shows the probability that someone who makes a new claim for Jobseeker's Allowance was last claiming that benefit less than six months previously. The data is taken from the spring quarters of the Joint Unemployment and Vacancies Operating System (JUVOS) cohort.

The second graph shows data for all employees in part-time and temporary jobs (shown separately) by reason for part-time and temporary employment. Data is for the spring quarter 2002 and is derived from the Labour Force Survey.

*Overall adequacy of the indicator: **medium**. While the claimant count data is sound, the narrower definition of unemployment that it represents means that it understates the extent of short-term working interspersed with spells of joblessness. The adequacy of the second graph can be regarded as high, as it is based on the LFS.*

Without access to training

Indicator
19

People with no qualifications are much less likely to receive some job-related training than those with some qualifications.

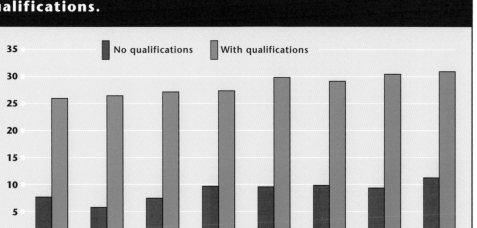

Source: LFS Spring Quarters, ONS 2002

The less qualified a person is, the less likely they are to receive job-related training.

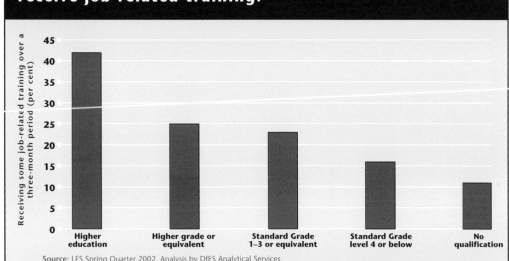

Source: LFS Spring Quarter 2002. Analysis by DfES Analytical Services

The first graph shows the proportion of employees of working age who have received some job-related training in the previous three months, according to whether they have some qualification or not. The qualifications include both current qualifications and qualifications which have been awarded in the past.

The second graph shows the proportion of employees of working age who have received training in the last three months according to the level of their highest educational qualification. As there are many possible qualifications, these have been grouped into a limited number of groups after taking advice from both the Scottish Executive and the Department for Education and Skills. Those who have a highest qualification which is not classifiable in the Labour Force Survey (around 5 per cent of the total) have not been shown on the graph on the grounds that they are likely to be a very disparate group.

In both cases, the date source is spring quarters of the Labour Force Survey (LFS) and the training includes that paid for by employers and by employees themselves.

*Overall adequacy of the indicator: **medium**. The LFS is a well-established, quarterly government survey of 60,000 households designed to be representative of the population as a whole. But a single, undifferentiated notion of 'training', without reference to its length or nature, can limit the clarity of the indicator.*

Commentary

Ethnic minorities and employment

Gina Netto, Scottish Ethnic Minorities Research Unit, Heriot Watt University, and Philomena de Lima, Inverness College

Scottish data on employment issues faced by minority ethnic groups is limited, fragmented and out-of-date, still being reliant on the 1991 Census and a large-scale general purpose survey of the minority ethnic population carried out by the Scottish Office in 1991. Both data sources are clearly out of date but continue to provide the basis for studies on employment issues.

In 1991, activity among the minority ethnic population was concentrated in a fairly narrow range of occupations and industries which are generally characterised by low pay and poor conditions of work, in particular the distribution, catering, hotel and repairs industries.

In addition, a higher proportion of minority ethnic householders worked in private companies and family businesses than white householders,[32] apparently supporting the observation that limited access to the labour market leads minority ethnic individuals to seek work in their own communities. The terms of such employment and pay are often informally negotiated, resulting in breaches in employment and pay legislation, and an acceptance of low pay, poor working conditions and exploitation.[33] Evidence on working conditions showed that on average minority ethnic employees worked longer hours and were more likely to work antisocial hours than their white counterparts.[34]

Second, self-employment was revealed to be the predominant form of employment amongst minority ethnic communities, with self-employment rates being five times higher for the minority ethnic population than for the white population.[35] There is conflicting evidence as to whether self-employment is a positive choice or an alternative route to employment. A study on enterprise development in minority ethnic communities found that, while discrimination was not perceived as the main motivating factor in entry decisions among entrepreneurs, it affected subsequent business development decisions.[36] In contrast, several studies suggest that self-employment is often the main alternative route into employment due to experience of discrimination in the labour market and limited occupational choice.[37]

Third, unemployment rates have consistently been higher in the minority ethnic population than the white population among both males and females, with the unemployment rate of minority ethnic females being double that of white females.[38] Factors which were more likely to increase the vulnerability of minority ethnic people to unemployment include ethnicity (unemployment rates were highest for Pakistanis at 26 per cent and lowest for Chinese at 8 1/2 per cent) and location (the rate was higher for Glasgow than the other Scottish cities).[39]

Finally, more recent studies show that, despite possessing higher educational qualifications, many minority ethnic youth encountered racial discrimination in their attempts to obtain employment.[40] Research has also shown that their participation in work and training schemes, including the New Deal Programme, is low. Many who do participate in such programmes do not find it a satisfactory experience. Of the 800 minority ethnic people aged 18 to 24 who entered the New Deal Programme between 1998 and 2000, a total of 540 subsequently left the scheme.[41] Young people's use of career advisory services is also low, a finding which has been attributed to lack of understanding of the service, its voluntary nature and users' negative experiences.[42]

The findings above support patterns identified in other parts of the UK, revealing a picture of racial inequality and divergence in the employment experiences of minority ethnic groups.[43] A recent survey showed that, while the vast majority of employer respondents stated that they had an equal opportunities policy in place, two-thirds of the employers were unable to demonstrate that steps had been taken to put equal opportunities policies into practice.[44] Minority ethnic employees, particularly women, were also more likely than their male colleagues to consider that discrimination had affected their working lives. Although studies of race equality policy and practice in the public and voluntary sector are lacking, it is likely that parallels may be drawn.

Other issues which have been highlighted in research and the work of the Scottish Trades Union Congress include harassment of minority ethnic employees by other employees and service users, and general feelings of dissatisfaction at opportunities for maximising individual potential and for progression within employment.[45]

Existing evidence of different patterns and racial inequality in employment strongly indicate the need for current, robust, ethnically disaggregated employment data in Scotland. Information on the constraints and opportunities facing minority ethnic groups in the labour market is also required.

In particular, there is a pressing need to evaluate the existence, nature and implementation of equal opportunities policies, with particular regard to employment in the public sector. Public sector organisations carry some responsibility for acting as models of good practice in this area and for influencing norms of practice in other sectors. The effective implementation and review of equal opportunities policies in employment practices would make a real difference to achieving racial equality, resulting in a workforce which is representative of the population. Not only is this integral to good personnel practice, but it is also likely to increase the accessibility and appropriateness of public services to the whole population. However, the effective implementation of such policies can only be achieved through commitment and accountability at the highest levels.

The argument for increasing the effectiveness of equal opportunities policies is further strengthened by the Race Relations (Amendment) Act 2000 which requires that all public sector employers subject to the general duty have a specific duty to monitor the ethnicity of staff in post and applicants for jobs, promotion and training. Public sector employers have a specific duty to monitor and analyse grievances, disciplinary action, performance appraisal, training, and dismissals and other reasons for leaving by ethnicity. The Act also requires them to publish annually the results of ethnic monitoring. An established public reporting framework which reports on progress made by public organisations in the recruitment, retention and progression of minority ethnic employees on an annual basis, as has been recently recommended,[46] would provide a sound basis for monitoring progress in employment equity in the public sector and for providing a baseline against which further progress in this area can be achieved.

Summary

Risk of low income

The risk of low income varies greatly depending on whether and how much paid work a household does. These risks have risen slightly, even for working households, over recent years. Among those in low income households, the proportion who are unemployed has fallen while the proportion who are working has risen.

Risk of unemployment

People with no qualifications are almost four times as likely to be unemployed as people with a higher education qualification. Among men under 25 and women under 20, the proportion who are unemployed is twice that for 25- to 44-year-olds.

Low attainment at school

Standard Grade attainment both for pupils on average and for the bottom 20 per cent has risen since 1995 but the gap between them remains. The proportion of 19-year-olds with either no or low qualifications is now back at the level of six years ago, after having risen and then fallen in the years in between.

Qualifications of school leavers

After falling between 1996 and 1998, the proportion of school leavers gaining no or low standard grades has remained static. There has been a big rise in the proportion leaving school with high standard grades. Pupils whose fathers are from manual backgrounds are more likely to get poor scores at Standard Grade than other pupils.

Destinations of school leavers

Over the last decade, while the proportion of school leavers entering higher or further education has risen steadily, the proportion entering training has more than halved. There are big variations between local authorities in the proportion of school leavers going into education, into training and into work.

Economic status of those of working age

The proportion of the working age population who are unemployed has been falling for at least a decade. The proportion who are economically inactive has only been falling since 1999. While the proportions of men and women who are unemployed both fall with age, the proportion of men who are economically inactive but would like work rises with age.

Households without work for two years or more

In 2002 more than 200,000 households had been workless for three years or more, the highest number in the past decade. Rates of economic inactivity among both men and women are higher in areas where the proportion of men who are unemployed is higher.

In receipt of Working Families Tax Credit

The introduction of WFTC has benefited all areas more or less equally, with about 3 per cent more people of working age claiming WFTC than claimed its predecessor Family Credit. The proportion claiming WFTC varies between local authorities, from just over 4 per cent to just under 12 per cent.

Blue-collar employment

An overall rise in jobs in Scotland in recent years masks a sharp fall in the number of jobs in industry and agriculture. While the total number of jobs in the industrial, agricultural and transport sectors changed little between 1995 and 2000, five local authority areas recorded losses of 10 per cent or more.

Low pay and pay inequalities

Earnings have become more unequal over the past decade, for both men and women. Depending on the industry, average hourly rates of pay for manual work are between 17 per cent and 28 per cent lower for women than for men.

Insecure work

Just under half the people making a new claim for Jobseeker's Allowance were last claiming less than six months ago. Only 1 in 10 part-time employees want a full-time job – but 4 in 10 temporary employees would like a permanent job.

Without access to training

People with no qualifications are much less likely to receive some job-related training than those with some qualifications. The less qualified a person is, the less likely they are to receive job-related training.

Chapter 3 Ill health

Theme	Indicator/map
Birth, death and disability	Indicator 20: Death rates for those aged 25 and 65
	Indicator 21: Long-standing illness or disability
	Indicator 22: Low birth-weight babies
Geography: Local concentrations of premature mortality	Map E: Standardised mortality rates for three diseases
	Indicator 23: Standardised mortality rates for three diseases
Health problems of young adults	Indicator 24: Suicides
	Indicator 25: Problem drug use

Birth, death and disability

Scotland enjoys the dubious distinction of having the second worst mortality rate in the European Union, better only than Portugal, the EU's poorest member, and worse than Northern Ireland by 10 per cent and England and Wales by almost 20 per cent.[1] This is not just a case of a few black spots dragging down an otherwise acceptable overall performance, since only Grampian, among Scotland's regions, has an all-age, social class, age and sex adjusted standardised mortality rate that is better than the England and Wales average.[2] If there is a saving grace, it is that the subject is now fully exposed to the public eye, with two recent reports in particular drawing attention to inequalities both within Scotland and between it and other countries.[3]

The concerns about health apply for all age groups. For adults and older people, rates of heart disease, stroke and cancer are high; mental health problems are also widespread.[4] For children and young people, there are concerns about poor diet, poor dental health (children in the West of Scotland have the worst record of dental health in Europe),[5] high rates of fatal pedestrian accidents (which for 10- to 14-year-olds are amongst the highest in Europe),[6] high rates of teenage conceptions, and a high incidence of mental health problems.[7] There are also concerns about drug use by young people and, in particular, about the circumstances of children in Scotland being cared for by drug using parents.

More specifically relating to this report, evidence of persisting inequalities in Scottish ill health are cause for considerable concern. Such inequalities relate both to income and social class. They arise from a range of factors, including greater risk of exposure to poor housing conditions and hazardous conditions at work, greater likelihood of adverse life circumstances and poorer health behaviours.[8] It has to be stressed these inequalities have persisted even while there are overall improvements in rates of serious disease and death.

Topics and indicators

The particular topics covered in this section range broadly across the different age groups, to highlight the problems that may apply at different stages of the life cycle. They are:

▌ Premature death.

▌ Limiting long-standing illness and disability.

▌ Low birth-weight babies.

Premature death is covered by an indicator [20a], measuring **the death rate of 65-year-olds**, with the result shown separately for men and women. Rates for 25-year-olds are also presented. In the supporting graph [20b] the indicator shows the standardised mortality rate for all under 65-year-olds broken down by social class, highlighting the health inequality evident in Scotland. Premature death is arguably the simplest, most accessible indicator for ill health, being a summary measure of all major health problems which result in death.

Limiting long-standing illness or disability is captured by an indicator [21a], showing the **number of adults aged 45 to 64 and 65 and over self-reporting a limiting long-standing illness, disability or infirmity**. In past Scottish Health Surveys, significant numbers of adults aged between 16 and 64 have reported having a long-standing illness or disability.[9] The supporting graph [21b] shows a breakdown of the **rates by tenure and age of self-reporting long-standing illness**.

Low birth-weight babies face a range of future health problems both immediate and longer term, including poor health in the first four weeks of life, a higher risk of death before the age of two and delayed physical and intellectual development in early childhood and adolescence. There is, again, a clear socio-economic pattern to the risk of low birth-weight babies. In addition their levels of occurrence indicate the way in which the historical disadvantage of children's parents can be transmitted from the very outset. The two graphs for this indicator [22] show **the proportion of babies with a low birth weight**, and a breakdown of **the rates for low birth-weight babies according to the deprivation category of their parents**.

What the indicators show

▌ Mortality rates for people aged 65 fell significantly during the 1990s, especially for men where the rate fell by almost a quarter. In contrast, the mortality rates for 25-year-olds of both sexes remained largely unchanged. [20a]

▌ The standardised mortality rate for people aged under 65 is on average twice as high in the most deprived 10 per cent of neighbourhoods as in the most prosperous 50 per cent. [20b]

▌ A quarter of both men and women aged 45 to 64 report a limiting long-standing illness or disability. The proportion rises to 2 in 5 among people aged 65 and over, with the rates for women slightly higher than those for men. [21a]

▌ The breakdown by tenure shows that the proportions reporting this condition are significantly higher among those in the social rented sector: 47 per cent of those aged 45 to 59 in that sector compared with 28 per cent among those in private rented accommodation and 18 per cent among owner occupiers. [21b]

▌ The higher incidence of this condition among those in the social rented sector applies for all age groups. So, for example, among those aged under 45, twenty-two per cent of those in the social rented sector report such a condition compared with 9 per cent among each of the other two tenure groups.

▌ At 2$^{1}/_{2}$ per cent, there has been little change in the proportion of babies with a low birth weight over the last decade [22a]. This is despite a variety of policy initiatives over this period aimed at reducing the incidence of low birth weights.[10]

▌ Analysis of low birth weight by the deprivation category ascribed to parents shows that, in 2001, babies born of parents who were most deprived were twice as likely to be of low birth weight compared with babies born of parents who were least deprived [22b]. This illustrates the persisting impact of poverty and deprivation on the risk of a baby being born with a low birth weight.

Other key points and relevant research

■ On all-cause mortality, Scotland is roughly in the middle of the league table of European countries. However, it lags behind most of the other Western European nations of similar wealth and stature, with only the poorer Eastern European nations having consistently worse mortality rates.[11]

■ Scotland's poor performance relative to the rest of the UK is highlighted by its lower life expectancy. From 1997–99, Scottish men could expect to live 2.3 years fewer than the UK male average and women 1.9 years fewer than the UK average.[12]

■ In the 1995 Scottish Health Survey, 35 per cent of the population aged 16 to 64 reported at least one long-standing illness or disability and 20 per cent stated that it limited their activities in some way.[13]

■ Data concerning pedestrian accidents amongst children in Scotland indicate that the poorest children are four times more likely to be killed in a road accident than the wealthiest. At home, they are nine times more likely to die in a fire.[14]

■ On average in Scotland, during a year, there are over 300 consultations for mental health problems for every 1,000 people in a general practice. Rates are fairly similar in most areas but are considerably higher in the most deprived areas.[15]

■ The rate of teenage conception in Scotland is the highest in Europe.[16] Teenage pregnancies in the most deprived areas are twice as likely to end in delivery as in affluent areas.[17]

■ Women in deprived areas are three times as likely to smoke during pregnancy as those in the least deprived areas.[18] Smoking in pregnancy poses risks to the baby, including having a low birth weight.[19]

■ Less than 30 per cent of children living in the most deprived areas are free of dental caries in comparison to 62 per cent of children living in the least deprived areas.[20]

Death rates for those
aged 25 and 65

Indicator
20

Mortality rates for 65-year-olds fell significantly over the 1990s, especially for men, where the rate dropped by almost a quarter; for 25-year-olds they have remained unchanged.

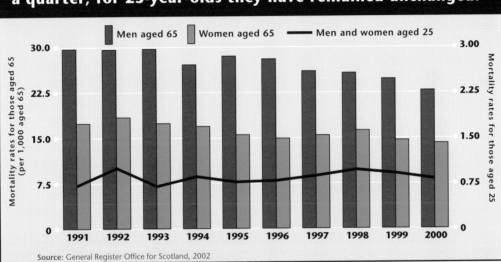

Source: General Register Office for Scotland, 2002

The standardised mortality rate for the under-65s is on average twice as high in the 10 per cent most deprived neighbourhoods as in the most prosperous 50 per cent.

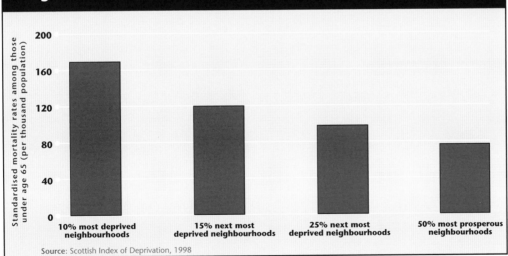

Source: Scottish Index of Deprivation, 1998

The first graph measures the death rate per 1,000 people aged 65, for men and women separately, over time. It also shows (on the Y axis on the right, drawn at 10 times the size in order to achieve legibility) the death rate per 1,000 people aged 25 for both sexes combined. Note that the population ratio of men to women for the years 1991 to 1997 is assumed to be the same as that between 1998 to 2000. The data is from the Scottish General Register Office.

The second graph shows the standardised mortality rate (SMR) of deaths from all causes by levels of geographic deprivation. It is standardised to the total Scottish population. An SMR of 100 suggests that local mortality rates are the same as national mortality rates when age and sex differences in the two populations are taken into account. Scores over 100 suggest higher than average mortality in an area, scores less than 100 lower than average mortality.

This graph is based on data from the 1998 area deprivation index published by the Central Statistics Unit. The data on SMRs, the population aged 16 to 65 and the index for each postcode sector is used to work out an average SMR (weighted by the population) for the 10 per cent most deprived, next 15 per cent most deprived, next 25 per cent most deprived and most prosperous 50 per cent, where deprivation/prosperity is per the deprivation index used in the Scottish Index of Deprivation.

*Overall adequacy of the indicator: **high**. Data on death rates and SMRs is sourced from administrative data and represents counts of all deaths.*

Long-standing illness or disability

**Indicator
21**

A quarter of people aged 45 to 64 have a limiting long-standing illness or disability. The proportion rises to two-fifths for those aged 65 and over.

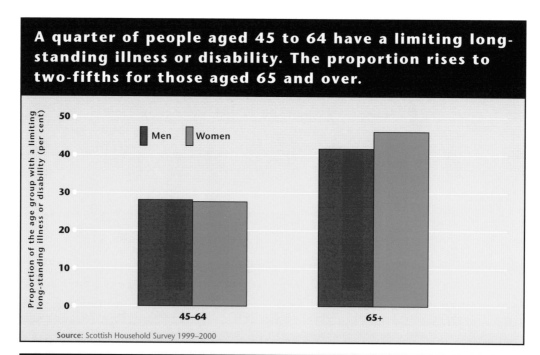

Source: Scottish Household Survey 1999–2000

People of all ages who are living in social rented accommodation are more likely to suffer from a limiting long-standing illness than those in other tenures.

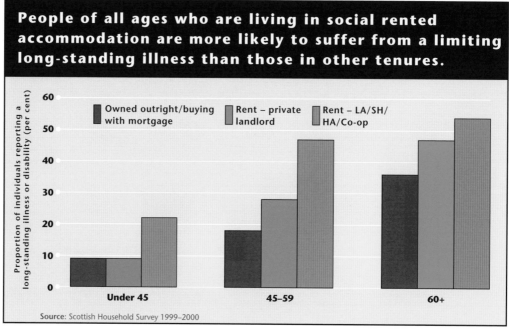

Source: Scottish Household Survey 1999–2000

The first graph shows the proportion of people aged 45 to 64 and 65-plus split by sex (shown separately) who report having a limiting long-standing illness or disability. This is a self-assessed measure and includes any limiting long-standing illness, health problem or disability.

The second graph shows the above data split by age band (under 45, 45–59 and 60-plus) and tenure.

Data for both graphs is from the Scottish Household Survey for 1999 and 2000 together.

Overall adequacy of the indicator: **high**. *The Scottish Household Survey is a large representative survey. See Indicator 1 for more details.*

Low birth-weight babies

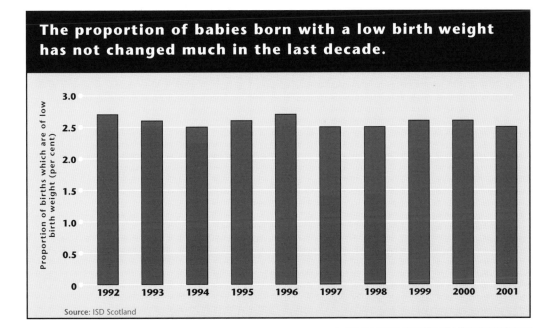

The proportion of babies born with a low birth weight has not changed much in the last decade.

Source: ISD Scotland

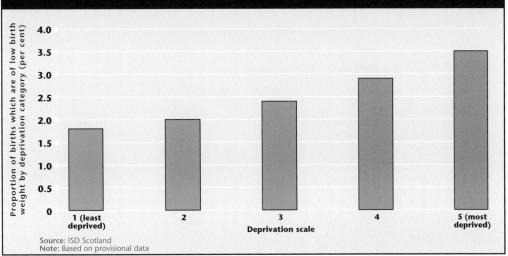

In 2001, babies born of parents who were most deprived were twice as likely to have a low birth weight compared with babies born of parents who are least deprived.

Source: ISD Scotland
Note: Based on provisional data

The first graph shows the percentage of babies born each year who are defined as having a low birth weight, i.e. less than 2.5 kilograms (5 1/2lbs). The data is for all full-term births for both singleton and multiple births. Note that data for 2001 was provisional at the time of publication. Home births and births at non-NHS hospitals are excluded.

The second graph shows the proportion of low birth-weight babies born in 2001 according to deprivation category of their parents' area of residence. Deprivation categories are based on data collected in the 1981 and 1991 census. A number of measures (overcrowding, male unemployment, low social class, no car) are combined to give a composite score for postcode sectors. There are five categories ranging from 1 (least deprived) to 5 (most deprived). The data omits those cases where deprivation category was not known.

*Overall adequacy of the indicator: The data is sourced from administrative data and represents a count of births. Adequacy for the second graph can be regarded as **medium**. Note that levels of deprivation in areas can change over time and the measure used may not adequately reflect this change. Also, this graph measures area deprivation, not deprivation of the parents themselves. Not everyone living in an area identified as deprived is necessarily deprived, and vice versa.*

Geography: Local concentrations of premature mortality

Variations in health outcomes across Scotland can be large, although they do not follow any simple pattern.[21] For example, within the Clydeside conurbation, the local authority with the poorest health outcomes in Scotland (Glasgow City) is bordered by two local authorities with the best health outcomes in Scotland (East Dunbartonshire and East Renfrewshire).[22] What this highlights is that variations in health status do not reflect a simple geographic divide – for example Glasgow versus the rest of Scotland – and that it is important to look at data at the local level since concentrations of extremely poor levels of health are not visible in summary national statistics.

Through the emerging body of research into health inequalities within the UK, and specifically within Scotland, there is growing evidence that inequalities in health are underpinned by variations in socio-economic deprivation. For example, analysis of death rates for specific diseases shows a clear pattern: in the most affluent areas, death rates are significantly below the Scottish average, whilst in the most deprived areas, they are significantly above the average.[23]

Work on the associations between health outcomes and markers of deprivation at the local authority level also reveals a pattern of positive association between poor health outcomes and higher levels of deprivation.[24] Growing evidence also suggests that while the individual socio-economic characteristics of the residents of an area are important, where people live also matters.

Topic, map and indicator

To reflect the importance of deprivation as a contributory factor in premature death, the focus of this section is on:

▮ Mortality rates due to diseases notable for their association with deprivation.

The map and the indicator are built around the average of the **standardised mortality rates (SMRs) for coronary heart disease, stomach cancer and cancer of the lung, bronchus and trachea**, this selection reflecting their connection with deprivation. Thus, rates for lung cancer among people living in the most deprived areas of Scotland are three times higher than in the least deprived areas. A similar pattern emerges for coronary heart disease, with those in the most deprived areas having a risk of dying that is two and a half times those in the least deprived areas.[25]

The map shows the ranks of 32 local authorities for the three SMRs combined, with the usual colour scheme applying, distinguishing between the four authorities with the highest count, the four with the next highest count, the next eight and the remaining 16. The supporting graph [23b] shows the value of these SMRs for each of the 32 local authorities.

The principal graph [23a] shows the count of the number of authorities annually since

1996 where **the combined SMR is 10 per cent or more above average**, with the number of authorities where it is 25 per cent or more above average shown separately. The interpretation of this graph is that a reduction in the number of authorities above 25 per cent, and a reduction in the total number above 10 per cent, would represent an improvement.

What the map and indicator show

▌ The four authorities with the highest SMRs are Inverclyde, Glasgow City, Dundee City and Falkirk. Among these four, the SMRs for the first two – 43 per cent and 30 per cent above average respectively – stand out. By contrast, the second two (at 16 per cent and 13 per cent above average) have rates only a little higher than those in the following group, namely Renfrewshire, East Lothian, Clackmannanshire and West Dunbartonshire. [23b and Map E]

▌ 18 authorities show rates below the average. With the exception of Orkney, where the rate is less than 50 per cent of the average, none of the other 17 authorities is more than 25 per cent below the average. [23b and Map E]

▌ In the five years 1996 to 2000, the number of authorities with SMRs for stomach cancer, lung cancer and heart disease that were more than 10 per cent above average fluctuated between eight and ten. [23a]

Other key points and relevant research

▌ The difference in male life expectancy between the most and least socio-economically disadvantaged local government districts in Scotland was 7.6 years in 2001 (Glasgow City had a life expectancy of 68.7 years, whereas East Renfrewshire was 76.3 years).[26]

▌ In 1998, mortality in Scotland was 16 per cent above the UK average. Seven of the worst ten UK local authorities for male life expectancy were in Scotland, as were four of the worst five authorities for female life expectancy.[27]

▌ Scotland has especially high rates of mortality from cancers and respiratory diseases. Its age-standardised mortality rate for all cancers in 1996 was 179 per 100,000 compared with 153 for England and Wales and a rate as low as 122 for Finland. Among 27 European countries, Scotland had the third highest rate below only those of the Czech Republic and Hungary.[28]

▌ By the age of 74, approximately 1 in 3 men and 1 in 4 women can expect to have been diagnosed with cancer.[29]

▌ Recent research has suggested that the serious economic decline experienced by areas such as Glasgow and Inverclyde might have 'impacted on population health status over and above the aggregate health status of poor individuals living within that area'.[30]

▌ Differences in health behaviour account for some of the health outcome inequalities between social classes. Forty-nine per cent of men in the most deprived areas smoke regularly compared with 26 per cent of men in the least deprived areas. The divide is similar for women: 43 per cent smoke in the most deprived areas, compared with 24 per cent in the least deprived.[31]

MAP E: The standardised mortality rates for stomach cancer, lung cancer and heart disease in the worst two areas – Inverclyde and Glasgow – are more than a third higher than in the average local authority area.

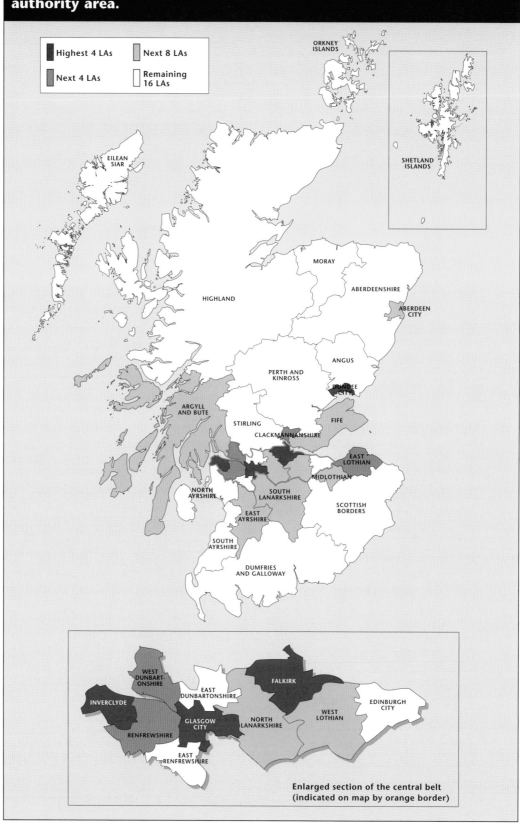

Standardised mortality rates for three diseases

The number of local authorities with combined standardised mortality rates for stomach cancer, lung cancer and heart disease that are well above average has not changed much over the past five years.

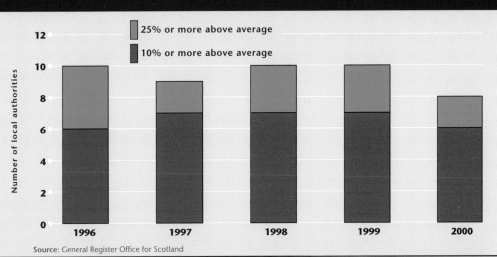

Source: General Register Office for Scotland

The standardised mortality rates for stomach cancer, lung cancer and heart disease in the worst two areas – Inverclyde and Glasgow – are more than a third higher than in the average local authority area.

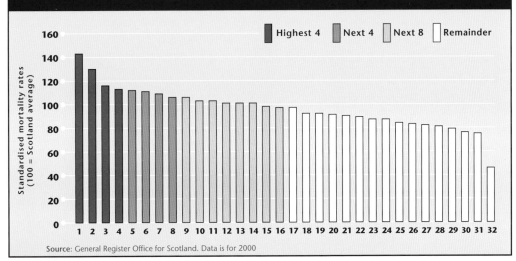

Source: General Register Office for Scotland. Data is for 2000

The first graph shows the number of local authorities where average standardised mortality rates (SMR) for stomach cancer, lung cancer and ischaemic heart disease is more than 10 per cent or 25 per cent above the national average (shown separately). The data is for 1996 to 2000, the earliest and latest years for which the data is available.

The second graph, which accompanies the map, shows the distribution of SMRs for deaths from the above causes by local authority. The local authorities are grouped into the top four in terms of highest SMR rates, the next four, the next eight and the remaining 16.

Data is standardised to the total Scottish population. An SMR of 100 suggests that local mortality rates are the same as national mortality rates when age and sex differences in the two populations are taken into account. Scores over 100 suggest higher than average mortality in an area, scores less than 100 lower than average mortality.

The data for both graphs is from the Scottish General Register Office.

*Overall adequacy of the indicator: **high**. Data on death rates and SMRs is sourced from administrative data and represents counts of all deaths.*

Health problems of young adults

The health of young adults in Scotland is a cause for concern for a number of reasons, including their use of drugs, their diet, rates of obesity, poor dental health and their mental health. Concerns about low levels of physical exercise and poor diet – specifically high intakes of saturated fat – have important associations with many of the diseases affecting adults in Scotland, which result in the high rates of premature death discussed earlier in this chapter.

Despite these serious health concerns, reports and policy initiatives – in both Scotland and England – have tended to focus on children under 16 to the detriment of older teenagers making the transition into adulthood. It is for this reason that young adults are identified as a distinct group within this report, with two indicators focused on health issues that are of particular relevance to them.

Topics and indicators

The indicators selected in this section pick up on possibly two of the most serious health issues facing young adults in Scotland that have the potential to end in early death. They are:

▌ Mental health.

▌ Drug misuse.

The importance of **mental health**, or well-being, is widely recognised in national reports and policy initiatives, although finding reliable measures of its prevalence is limited by the fact that much of the available data is of either a self-reporting or an administrative kind – for example, hospital admission rates – and, as such, fails to pick up on the hidden morbidity of those with mental health problems who have failed to come to the attention of service providers. Similar arguments apply for drug misuse.

Two sources of data relating to mental health are presented: a graph showing **suicides amongst young adults aged between 15 and 24** over time [24a] and a graph showing **the risk of developing a mental illness (for all ages)** [24b] separately for men and women. Whilst acknowledging that there are many factors relating to suicide and that, as such, it cannot be used as a direct measure of mental health, suicide data is presented here as a proxy measure since it is an important cause of premature death amongst young men in Scotland.[32]

Drug misuse amongst young teenagers is a particular concern in Scotland. Early usage of drugs is also more likely to be associated with later addiction and mental health problems. The data presented for this indicator shows, first, **the numbers of young adults aged 15-24 starting a drug treatment episode** [25a] and, second, a presentation of this data broken down by **the employment status of young people starting a drug treatment episode.** [25b]

What the indicators show

▮ The number of recorded suicides among young adults between 15 and 24 has fluctuated at around 120 per year for the last decade. However, since the number of people in that age group fell by a sixth over that period, this represents a rising rate of suicides among this age group. [24a]

▮ Based on evidence from the 1999 Scottish Health Survey, 1 in 5 women and 1 in 8 men are identified as at risk of developing a mental illness. [24b]

▮ The number of young adults starting a drug treatment episode has been broadly stable over the last five years, averaging around 4,000 people a year. About two-thirds of those starting such an episode are men. [25a]

▮ Four-fifths of young adults aged 15 to 25 starting a drug treatment episode are unemployed, of which a sixth have never been employed. [25b]

Other key points and relevant research

▮ Recent research suggests that suicides are twice as common in the most deprived areas of Scotland and that, over the last decade, rates have increased more in the most deprived areas.[33]

▮ The suicide rate in Scotland for 15- to 24-year-olds is now roughly double the rate in England and Wales. By contrast, a decade ago, the rate was very much closer to that of England and Wales. Over the intervening period, while the number of suicides in Scotland has remained largely unchanged, the number in England and Wales has fallen by a third.[34]

▮ Data from the Scottish Schools Survey 2000 reveals that 22 per cent of 15-year-olds reported drug use in the previous month and 30 per cent in the previous year. Cannabis was by far the most likely drug to have been used.[35]

▮ Survey data for Glasgow in 1997 found that 14 per cent of males aged 18 to 23 were overweight or obese.[36]

▮ Around 80 young people in Scotland under the age of 16 become homeless every day, and each year around 11,500 young people aged between 16 and 24 apply to their local authority as homeless, for housing support.[37]

Suicides

There have been around 120 suicides amongst young adults aged 15 to 24 in most years since 1992.

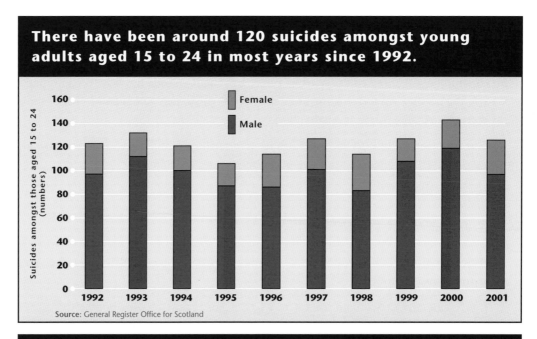

Source: General Register Office for Scotland

1 in 5 women and 1 in 8 men are assessed to be at risk of developing a mental illness.

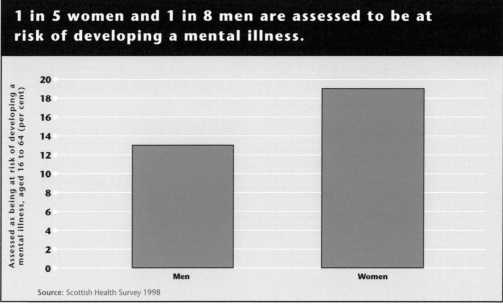

Source: Scottish Health Survey 1998

The first graph shows the number of suicides committed by young adults aged 15 to 24, split by sex. Data for 2001 is the latest available. The data is from the Scottish General Register Office.

The second graph shows proportions of people aged 16 to 64 who are assessed as having a potential psychiatric disorder. High risk is determined by asking informants a number of questions about general levels of happiness, depression, anxiety, stress and sleep disturbance over the past few weeks, which are designed to detect possible psychiatric morbidity. A score is constructed from the responses, and the figures published show those with a score of 4 or more. This is referred to as a 'high GHQ12 score'.

The data is from the Scottish Health Survey and is 1998 data (the latest available).

Overall adequacy of the indicator: **high**. *Data on suicides is sourced from administrative data collected by the Scottish General Register Office and is thought to be reliable. Data for the second graph can be regarded as medium. The graph does not measure mental ill health directly, but provides a guide to numbers who display some of the symptoms and are therefore at risk.*

Problem drug use

**In 2000/01, around four thousand young people aged
15 to 24 presented for treatment for drug misuse, a
similar number to five years ago.**

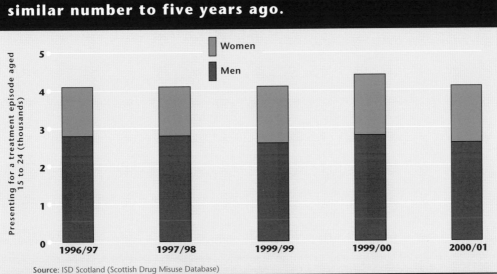

Source: ISD Scotland (Scottish Drug Misuse Database)

**The vast majority of young adults aged 15 to 24
presented for a treatment episode are unemployed, and
a substantial number have never been employed.**

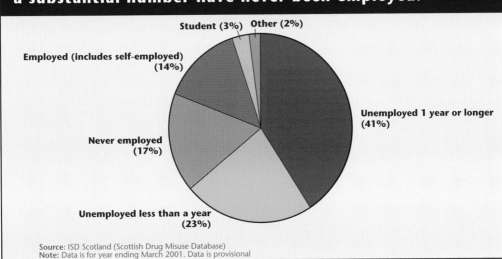

Source: ISD Scotland (Scottish Drug Misuse Database)
Note: Data is for year ending March 2001. Data is provisional

The first graph shows the number of 'new' individuals aged 15 to 24 presenting for treatment with agencies that offer services to drug misusers and report to the Scottish Drug Misuse Database. The annual analysis includes the first occurrence of individuals within each year. Data is for 1996/97 to 2000/01 – the earliest and latest for which the data is available.

The second graph shows the breakdown for the same data for 2000/01 by employment status.

The data source for both graphs is the Scottish Drugs Misuse Database.

*Overall adequacy of the indicator: **limited**. The numbers count individuals presenting for treatment in each six-month period, but do not include those in treatment who presented in an earlier six-month period. Furthermore, services such as needle exchange schemes, outreach work and most services for those in prison are excluded. Finally many problem drug users do not present for treatment at all.*

Commentary

Health and inequality in Scotland

Ken Judge, University of Glasgow

The average level of health of people in Scotland is relatively poor when compared with other parts of the UK and with countries in the European Union. One of the main reasons for this health record is the perpetuation of health inequalities between rich and poor people and communities within Scotland. With few exceptions, marked differences in behaviour, disease, disability and premature death are associated with area deprivation, household poverty and occupational social class. In short, inequalities in social circumstances are significantly reducing Scotland's health potential. It is possible that other factors such as climate may also contribute to Scotland's low position in the European health league table, but there can be no escaping the unacceptable fact that social injustice causes preventable illness and avoidable mortality.

Research clearly demonstrates that health inequalities exist between communities and individuals across the whole of Scotland and that large numbers of people are affected.[38] While most of these inequalities are the consequence of the poor social circumstances of individuals and families, where they live is also important. Disadvantaged people may have worse health partly because they live in places that are health damaging. For example, many parts of the west of Scotland have suffered massive industrial dislocation in recent decades that has severely affected the economic, physical and social infrastructure of many communities, in health-damaging ways.

Despite these facts becoming increasingly well known, there are severe difficulties to be faced in addressing them. It is not always clear which of the many hundreds of manifestations of health inequalities are of greatest significance. There is little evidence about trends over time in socially determined variations in health. Perhaps most significantly of all, there is a real absence of good evidence about how best to invest in policies that will reduce health inequalities. As a result, there is growing disquiet that many well-intentioned policies to invest in health improvement plans are not making sufficient progress because of the lack of a clear focus about priorities and the availability of good quality data to monitor trends.

Part of the problem is that health inequality is not a simple concept that can be examined through a single lens. It can be measured in a wide variety of ways, for example, by linking age, gender, ethnicity or place of residence with such diverse health indicators as infant mortality, teenage pregnancy, drug abuse, smoking behaviour, access to primary health care, cancer survival and many others. At the same time, there is too much reliance on simple measures of inequality like the absolute or relative differences between the best and worst social classes or deprivation categories. It would make more sense to evaluate the distribution of health across the whole population. Better analysis of data about the health and social circumstances of clearly defined social groups would also be useful to facilitate the monitoring of trends in health inequalities and their determinants. But – no matter how sophisticated the scrutiny of trends in health outcomes for disadvantaged populations becomes – new forms of information on their own will not be sufficient to achieve change.

At present, too many social initiatives encourage the dissipation of scarce resources. This is because public agencies often adopt a scattergun approach in seeking to alleviate the problems of isolated groups of disadvantaged people in disconnected ways. Health boards, for example, claim to be using new finance to tackle health inequalities without being able to mount any convincing evidence of what the impact of their interventions might be. Similarly, local authorities have real difficulty in demonstrating how they will achieve desired outcomes from special allocations of finance that are meant to foster a social justice agenda.

What is needed is a clearer sense of strategic direction about how to promote a fairer distribution, and a higher average level, of health for the people of Scotland. To help achieve this, a focused debate is needed to try to build a consensus about which aspects of health inequalities are most significant for which social groups and to determine which statistical indicators should be used to monitor progress. If a manageable basket of indicators could be produced then there would be a more realistic prospect of achieving two important goals. First, health and social policies themselves could be designed and implemented in a more focused way that offered some greater prospect of success. Second, it would be possible to monitor and comment on progress being made in a more informative way than is possible at the present time.

There can be no doubt whatsoever that the Scottish Parliament and its Executive are genuinely committed to reducing health inequality. But the time is fast approaching when rhetoric must be replaced by clearer action. Future approaches to promoting a step change in Scotland's health must be much more focused so that progress in promoting social justice can be reviewed in a more meaningful way.

The emphasis on socio-economic determinants of health inequalities in the social justice strategy provides an excellent starting point. But there is a real concern that, although the 'prescription' for change is the right one, the 'dose' is too weak. Much of the responsibility for this lies with Westminster rather than Holyrood. For example, any serious attempt to reduce inequality requires radical changes to tax and benefit policies that are not devolved powers. Within the realm of health policy, however, the Scottish Executive has more room for manoeuvre. What is badly needed is a firm commitment to specific health inequality targets and a health improvement plan that clearly sets out how these might be achieved.

Summary

Death rates for those aged 25 and 65

Mortality rates for 65-year-olds fell significantly over the 1990s, especially for men where the rate dropped by almost a quarter. The mortality rate for 25-year-olds has remained unchanged. The standardised mortality rate for the under 65s is on average twice as high in the 10 per cent most deprived neighbourhoods as in the most prosperous 50 per cent.

Long-standing illness or disability

A quarter of people aged 45 to 64 have a limiting long-standing illness or disability. The proportion rises to two-fifths for those aged 65 and over. People of all ages who are living in social rented accommodation are more likely to suffer from a limiting long-standing illness than those in other tenures.

Low birth-weight babies

The proportion of babies born with a low birth weight has not changed much in the last decade. Babies born of parents who are most deprived are twice as likely to be of low birth weight compared with babies born of parents who are least deprived.

Standardised mortality rates for three diseases

The number of local authorities with combined standardised mortality rates for stomach cancer, lung cancer and heart disease that are well above average has not changed much over the past five years. The standardised mortality rates for stomach cancer, lung cancer and heart disease in the worst two areas – Inverclyde and Glasgow – are more than a third higher than in the average local authority area.

Suicides

There have been around 120 suicides amongst young adults aged 15 to 24 in most years since 1992. One in 5 women and 1 in 8 men are assessed to be at risk of developing a mental illness.

Problem drug use

In 2000/01, around four thousand young people aged 15 to 24 started treatment for drug misuse, a similar number to five years ago. The vast majority of young adults aged 15 to 24 starting a treatment episode are unemployed, and a substantial number have never been employed.

Chapter 4 Quality of life and social cohesion

Theme	Indicator/map
Housing: Access, quantity and quality	Indicator 26: Homeless households
	Indicator 27: Affordable housing
	Indicator 28: Households without central heating
Quality of services	Indicator 29: Satisfaction with services
	Indicator 30: Satisfaction with public transport
	Indicator 31: Without a bank or building society account
Community	Indicator 32: Satisfaction with local area
	Indicator 33: Participation in the community
	Map F: Voting
	Indicator 34: Voting

Housing: Access, quantity and quality

The physical conditions in which people live, and whether or not they have secure, permanent accommodation, have a considerable impact on their well-being. They affect health, both mental and physical, relations between household members and child development. A lack of affordable, suitable housing manifests itself in many ways, including overcrowding and homelessness. Homelessness is a wider issue than rough sleeping – rough sleepers only account for a small proportion of homeless people[1] – and it is always a serious problem. For example, the insecurity and stress associated with homelessness are especially apparent when children are housed in inappropriate accommodation, such as bed and breakfast.[2]

Many of the issues to do with quality of the housing stock come together in the problem of fuel poverty, which is officially defined as being when a household has to spend at least 10 per cent of its income on fuel in order to maintain a satisfactory heating regime.[3] Fuel poverty therefore captures three things: the use of inefficient means of heating homes; poorly insulated buildings; and the extent to which these first two problems are concentrated among low income households. The matter has recently been the subject of a special 'statement' from the Scottish Executive, reflecting and developing the UK government's fuel poverty strategy.

Topics and indicators

The indicators in this section address the following three aspects of the quantity and quality of the housing stock:

I Homelessness and the availability of suitable housing.

I The availability of affordable housing.

I The standard of housing.

The indicator chosen to represent *homelessness* is **the number of households assessed as being homeless or potentially homeless [26a]**. The supporting graph [26b] shows the **extent of overcrowding by tenure** using a measure of occupation density known as the 'bedroom standard'. This takes account of the number of bedrooms in the dwelling, the number of people living there, their relationship to one another, and their age. The graph shows figures for different tenures separately.

Data relating to *the availability of affordable housing* is scarce. As a proxy measure, Indicator 27a is **the number of new lets allocated by public authorities** (i.e. local authorities, new towns or Scottish Homes) where 'new lets' are those to people who were not previously tenants (in other words, excluding transfers). By way of background, the graph also shows the trend in the proportion of all dwellings in Scotland that are in the social rented sector, with the figures for housing associations shown separately.

The supporting graph [27b] shows **the share of homes in the social and private rented**

sectors separately for a range of different urban and rural areas. This choice reflects a concern that the availability of affordable housing is a particular problem in rural areas.

In view of its importance, the obvious choice for an indicator on *the standard of housing* would be one which measures fuel poverty. However, with no reliable data on this subject currently available,[4] the chosen indicator [28a] is instead one measuring **the proportion of households without central heating**, with numbers shown separately for those on low income. This subject is important in its own right, with clear commitments from the Scottish Executive to have central heating installed in all housing in the social rented sector except Glasgow by 2004, and in Glasgow by 2006.[5] The interpretation of this statistic is therefore clear, although the variable quality and efficiency of central heating systems should also be borne in mind.

The supporting graph [28b] provides a breakdown of the **homes lacking central heating by the type of accommodation** and whether it is rented, owned outright, or is being bought with a mortgage.

What the indicators show

▌ The number of households assessed as homeless or potentially homeless rose in both the early and later years of the 1990s, from 24,000 in 1990/91 to 34,000 in 1999/2000. Throughout the period the number of applicants to be considered as homeless was about 12,000 more than the number assessed. [26a]

▌ The percentage of homes that are overcrowded is highest among those who rent their homes (over 5 per cent) and lowest (1½ per cent) among those who own their homes outright. Levels of overcrowding in rented accommodation are similar for both private landlords and local authorities. [26b]

▌ Over the 1990s, the share of properties provided by public authorities declined by more than a third, from 38 to 24 per cent, while the share for the social rented sector as whole (including housing associations) fell by a quarter, from 40 to 30 per cent. These declines reflect the sale of council houses under right-to-buy legislation. [27a]

▌ At under 20 per cent of the local housing stock, the share of social rented accommodation in both 'accessible' and 'remote' rural areas is lower than in urban areas and small towns, where the percentage is above 30. In all areas, the amount of social rented accommodation is substantially greater than the amount of private rented accommodation. [27b]

▌ In spite of the large fall in its overall stock of dwellings, the annual number of new lets made by public authorities between 1992 and 1999 showed no downward trend, fluctuating in the low 40,000s. The figure was, however, higher in 1991 and (after a gap in the data) lower again in 2002, at 37,000. [27a]

▌ The proportion of households without central heating has been falling sharply over recent years, to 8 per cent (for all households) and 13 per cent (for households with a gross weekly income of under £200) in 1999/2000. The comparable figures five years earlier were 17 and 25 per cent respectively. Indeed the percentage for those who were poor in 1999/2000 was actually lower than the percentage for the average just four years earlier. [28a]

▌ Flats are at least twice as likely to lack central heating as houses. Within each type of dwelling, the likelihood is highest for those that are rented and lowest for those that are being bought with a mortgage. [28b]

Other key points and relevant research

▌ Until the passage of the Housing (Scotland) Act 2001, local authorities had an obligation to provide temporary accommodation only to those households deemed to be in 'priority need', of which the most common reason for a household's application being accepted is the presence of dependent children (44 per cent of cases in 1999/2000).[6] The 2001 Act means that local authorities now have an obligation to provide at least temporary accommodation for all households accepted as homeless.

▌ The average duration of homelessness (measured as the length of stay in temporary accommodation) varies according to the type of accommodation in which the household is placed. For 2000/01, the average stay was 64 days in hostels, 123 days in temporary council furnished accommodation, 26 days in bed and breakfast and 153 days in other accommodation.[7]

▌ The possibility that rural authorities' capacity to respond to homelessness is constrained by the lack of 'affordable' housing is demonstrated by the greater probability that households deemed to be in priority need are placed in temporary accommodation (63 per cent in rural areas as opposed to 51 per cent in urban authorities) and the heightened likelihood of being accommodated in bed and breakfast accommodation (21 per cent compared with 7 per cent).[8]

▌ Overcrowding appears to be twice as prevalent among minority ethnic households as among white ones although, at 10 and 5 per cent respectively, only a small minority are in this situation.[9]

▌ Fuel poverty in Scotland is widespread: almost 750,000 (equivalent to 1 in every 3) homes were suffering from it in 1996, of whom 180,000 were in 'extreme' fuel poverty, spending more than 20 per cent of their income on fuel.[10]

▌ The balance between the numbers renting their home and the numbers owning it has changed substantially in the last decade, with owner occupation rising from 52 to 63 per cent. This is, however, still below the English 2000/01 level of 70 per cent.[11]

▌ Minority ethnic households are disproportionately under-represented in the rented sector. Research evidence documents barriers to the social rented sector, including discrimination, allocation criteria and lack of publicity about the availability of such accommodation within minority ethnic communities.[12]

Homeless households

Indicator
26

The number of households assessed as homeless or potentially homeless rose by 50 per cent during the 1990s.

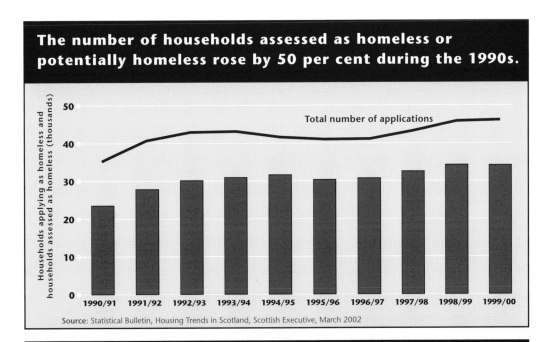

Source: Statistical Bulletin, Housing Trends in Scotland, Scottish Executive, March 2002

Households in rented accommodation are one and a half times more likely to be overcrowded than those who are buying their home with a mortgage.

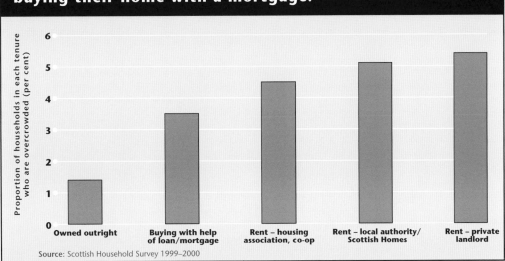

Source: Scottish Household Survey 1999–2000

The first graph shows the total number of applications to local authorities made by households under the Homeless Persons Legislation and, of those, the numbers assessed as homeless or potentially homeless by the local authority for each of the years shown. Application figures will include some households that have applied more than once during the year. The data is from the Scottish Executive.

The second graph shows the number of households that are overcrowded, split by tenure. Overcrowding is defined as households that fall below a measure of occupation density known as the 'bedroom standard'. The 'bedroom standard' is calculated in relation to the number of bedrooms, the number of household members and their relationship to each other. One bedroom is allocated to each married or cohabiting couple, any other person over 21, each pair aged 10 to 20 of the same sex and each pair of children under 10.

Note that the graph omits 'other' households not covered by any of the classifications shown. This category amounts to 2.2 per cent of households.

The data is from the Scottish Household Survey, for 1999 and 2000 together.

*Overall adequacy of the indicator: **medium**. While there is no reason to believe there is any problem with the underlying data, the extent to which it leaves 'homelessness' dependent on administrative definition is restrictive. In particular, the figures do not include any single people, towards whom local authorities have no general duty. Also, not all homeless people apply to local authorities.*

Affordable housing

Indicator 27

The annual number of new lets by public authorities remained in the 40,000s during the 1990s, although the total stock of public housing declined by more than a third.

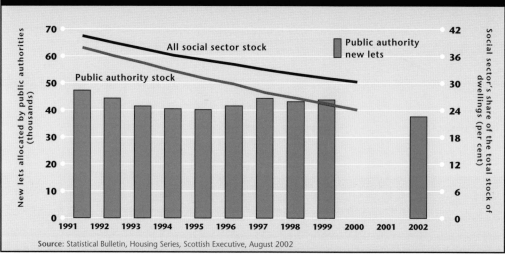

Source: Statistical Bulletin, Housing Series, Scottish Executive, August 2002

Social rented accommodation is a smaller proportion of the housing stock in rural areas than urban areas.

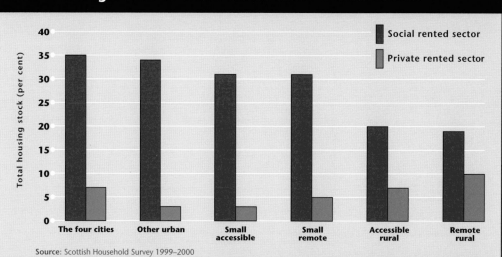

Source: Scottish Household Survey 1999–2000

The first graph measures the number of new lets allocated by public authorities (i.e. local authorities, new towns or Scottish Homes). This is represented on the graph by the bars and the left-hand Y axis. 'New lets' are those to people who were not previously tenants (in other words, excluding transfers). The graph also shows the proportion of all dwellings that are the social rented sector, with the figures for housing associations shown separately. This is represented by the lines and the right-hand Y axis.

The data sources is the Scottish Executive Bulletin, Housing Series.

The second graph shows housing tenure by area type (rural to urban). It shows the proportion of the total housing stock that is from the social and private rented sectors (shown separately). This is drawn from a longer list of tenure types. The data source is the Scottish Household Survey for 1999 and 2000 together.

The area types are as follows: 'four cities' (Glasgow, Edinburgh, Dundee and Aberdeen); 'other urban': population between 10,000 and 125,000; 'small accessible': population between 3,000 to 10,000 and within 30 minutes' drive of a settlement of more than 10,000; 'small remote': population between 3,000 to 10,000 and more than 30 minutes' drive of a settlement of more than 10,000; 'accessible rural': population less than 3,000 and within 30 minutes' drive of a settlement of more than 10,000; and 'remote rural': population less than 3,000 and more than 30 minutes' drive of a settlement of more than 10,000.

*Overall adequacy of the indicators: **high**. Data on dwelling stocks is based on administrative data collected by the Scottish Executive and therefore represents a count of total dwellings.*

Households without central heating

Households with a low income are more likely than average to lack central heating, but the numbers have been coming down sharply.

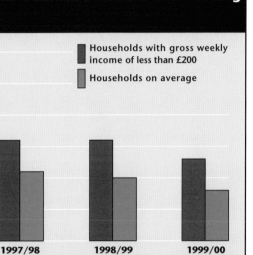

Source: The Family Resources Survey, ONS 1999/2000

Those living in rented flats are much less likely to have central heating than those living in houses they own or are buying with a mortgage.

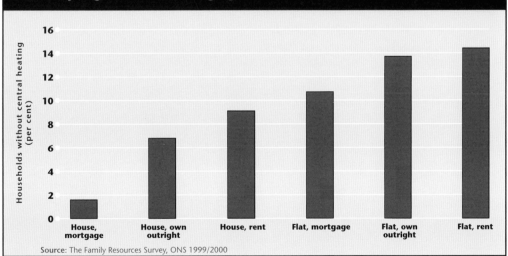

Source: The Family Resources Survey, ONS 1999/2000

The first graph shows the proportion of households without central heating, with separate figures for households with a gross weekly income of less than £200 and all households. Data is shown for the years 1995/96 to 1999/00 – the earliest and latest years respectively for which the data is available.

The second graph shows data for 1999/00 split by tenure.

Data for both graphs is taken from the Family Resources Survey with analysis by the New Policy Institute.

*Overall adequacy of the indicator: **high**. The FRS is a well-established government survey that gathers information on household incomes and other resources. It is designed to be representative of the population as a whole.*

Commentary

Housing in rural areas

Mark Shucksmith, University of Aberdeen

Rural housing markets: tenure and affordability

Overall, 61 per cent of housing in rural[13] Scotland is owner-occupied, compared with 56 per cent in urban areas. Rural Scotland also has a much smaller social rented sector (26 per cent compared with 38 per cent in urban areas). Since 1990, there has been an overall decline both in the private rented sector and in the social rented sector, the latter primarily due to the mandatory sale of council houses. The relative importance of the private market in allocating houses is one legacy of difference between rural and non-rural areas, and its concomitant, the lack of social housing, has been widely identified as one of the most important issues facing rural communities.[14]

Housing markets in rural areas are not 'free-markets', of course. On the demand side, the general tendency towards smaller households is augmented in more pressured rural areas by the purchase of retirement and holiday homes, and/or by commuters seeking the perceived benefits of a rural lifestyle. The population of rural Scotland is growing, in aggregate, while the urban population falls. It is on the supply side, though, that regulation imposes constraints through the planning system and policies of urban containment.[15] Planning is (ab)used as an 'instrument of social exclusivity'[16] through which the interests of the most powerful are imposed on the weak. The importance of land ownership constraints on housing provision in some rural areas of Scotland has also been noted as an instance of market failure in land markets, and thus in housing markets. It should be emphasised that the Scottish Executive is aware of these issues.[17]

Who is affected?

Because of the over-emphasis on owner occupation and the concomitant lack of housing to rent, especially social housing, there is a lack of choice within rural housing markets for those who do not have the means to compete effectively within the private sector. For these households and individuals, the allocation of houses through the state and voluntary sectors is crucial to their chances of finding an affordable home. Analysis of council allocations and waiting lists in rural Scotland[18] identified those most favoured by the allocation criteria (families with children) and those most likely to be excluded (young single people, young couples and, to a lesser extent, older people). Young families and single person households are often seen by residents as having the most restricted housing choice in rural areas.

Councils are now under considerable pressure from central government to transfer their stock to housing associations.[19] Meanwhile, housing associations' central aim of meeting housing needs has sat uneasily at times beside the priorities of their funding agency (then Scottish Homes), particularly over the level of rents to be charged and the balance between the affordable rented programme and building for low-cost home ownership.[20]

Poor quality housing

There is also a problem of the quality of housing in rural Scotland. In 1990, there were an estimated 24,700 properties 'below tolerable standard' in rural Scotland, with rural households being three times more likely to live in such a home than the Scottish average.[21] The estimated cost of repairs was £412 million. Much of this poor housing was damp, insufficiently maintained, and in the private sector. In rural Scotland, '1 in 8 dwellings experience dampness; 1 in 4 experience condensation; and 1 in 4 have poor energy ratings. A higher proportion of rural housing was built before 1919'.[22]

Previous efforts to tackle rural disrepair had been less effective than in urban areas largely because no appropriate strategy had been developed or pursued. Elderly and poor households were most likely to be living in damp or otherwise unsuitable dwellings[23] and many were unable to afford the cost of the improvements needed. Private landlords were often reluctant to carry out improvements due to the large capital outlay required and the poor returns.

Key issues

Key issues emerging in rural areas of Scotland are therefore:

I Supply-side constraints, notably planning regulation and monopoly land ownership.

I Increasing demand, both from external sources and from smaller household size.

I The declining stock of affordable social housing, both because of the right to buy and because of severe cutbacks in public investment.

I The small and expensive private rented sector, which is also declining.

I The poor physical condition of private housing in rural areas.

Data and monitoring

Systematic evidence of these phenomena is poor, with our understanding largely derived from academic research and one-off surveys. The Scottish Household Survey has potential but a larger sample size would be necessary to monitor trends at levels below local authority area.[24]

Ideally, the following indicators at postcode sector level would allow progress to be monitored:

I *Affordability*: for example, the Countryside Agency (2002) compiles an index of affordability for England using data from the New Earnings Survey and house prices from the Land Registry.

I *Rent levels* by tenure.

I *Social housing* for rent as a proportion of all dwellings.

I *Investment* in new social housing for rent by Communities Scotland.

I *House conditions*, including presence of dampness and condensation.

Quality of services

Inequalities in the standard of service provision between deprived and other neighbourhoods both reflect and exacerbate economic disadvantage.[25] If services are of a poor quality, more prosperous households will be less inclined to move into, or remain in, the area. Inequality in service provision also compounds the difficulty of living on a low income because people in more deprived areas are more likely to be dependent on public services and so suffer more from their poorer quality. Providers of public services in disadvantaged areas can face difficulties such as recruitment and retention of staff and, in welfare related provision, high demand.[26] Tackling unequal outcomes in local public service provision is part of the Scottish Executive's approach to regenerating deprived communities and reducing the gap between neighbourhoods,[27] with expenditure targeted at investment in public services in the more disadvantaged local authorities.[28]

Accessibility is a particular aspect of service quality which encompasses a number of important issues, including both what is provided locally (for example, a local health centre and the services offered there) and the adequacy of public transport links to reach other, larger centres. This is not just a matter of public services, whether delivered by a public authority such as the health service, or by a private company as in the case of public transport. It also applies to private services, for example whether there is a local chemist and (if not) whether specialist goods like baby milk are nevertheless available locally.[29] Issues of accessibility also apply to private services like banking, including whether the bank has a local branch, whether people on lower incomes are as numerous among the banks' customers as people on average, and whether services are tailored to the needs of people with low incomes.

In its turn, this last issue of suitability applies much more widely, especially for some minority ethnic people – for example, the need for culturally responsive social care services (such as the employment of bilingual workers and interpreters or the development of non-traditional arrangements to support elderly people in their homes); or the central importance of information and good communication more generally throughout health service provision.[30]

Topics and indicators

The indicators in this section explore:[31]

▌ Perceptions of the quality of local services.

▌ The extent to which people on a low income are well served by private services.

Perceptions of the quality of local services is covered by two indicators. The first of these [29a] measures **the proportion of people dissatisfied with the overall level of service provided by their local council**, with the results broken down according to the respondent's occupation. This is supported by an indicator [29b] illustrating perceptions of **the convenience of local services**, namely the doctor, the post office and the local shop, broken down by a six category urban–rural hierarchy, stretching from the four cities at one end, to remote rural areas on the other.

The indicator of satisfaction with public transport [30a] measures **the proportion of people who found public transport either fairly or very inconvenient**, with the results broken down into the same six category 'urban–rural hierarchy'. This choice reflects the recognition that inadequate public transport has received within the Scottish Executive, who see it as one of the major causes of social exclusion within rural communities[32]. It is supported by an indicator [30b], again broken down by the 'urban–rural hierarchy', showing the relative importance of different reasons given by people for being non-users of public transport.

The extent to which low income people are well served by private services is represented by an indicator [31a] which measures **the proportion of people lacking a bank or building society account**, with the results shown over time and separately for people on average and people on low income. Lack of an account can mean limited access to credit and so greater financial vulnerability, labour market disadvantage (employers tend to expect to pay wages directly into accounts) and higher prices for basic utilities than those paying by either cheque or direct debit.[33] The Scottish Executive is committed to extending access to financial services, in so far as its powers permit.[34] Access to financial services is also indicative of wider issues relating to essential private sector services.

This is supported by an indicator [31b] which shows **the proportions lacking household contents insurance**, broken down by the 'Mosaic' classification, which combines income, tenure, household and area (rural/urban) characteristics, ranging from 'high income areas' to 'families in council flats'.

What the indicators show

■ The view that councils do not provide high quality services is held by around one in three people in Scotland. Rates of dissatisfaction are highest among those from manual and lower skilled backgrounds, and lowest among those from professional backgrounds. [29a]

■ The problem of inconvenient post offices and shops is most common among those in rural areas outside small towns, where typically around 1 in 6 describe them as inconvenient. There is no such pattern to the proportion who report that they find doctor services inconvenient. [29b]

■ Problems with public transport are felt particularly strongly in rural areas outside small towns, with 40 per cent of people in accessible rural areas – and 50 per cent in remote rural areas – judging it to be inconvenient. By contrast, the figure for small towns is 20 per cent and only 10 per cent for large urban areas. [30a]

■ Among those who cannot use public transport to go to work or school, the infrequency of services is more of a problem in remote rural areas (including small towns), whereas slow journey times are perceived as a greater problem in urban areas and, to some extent, in accessible rural areas. [30b]

■ People in poor households are far more likely to lack both a bank and a building society account than people on average: 30 per cent compared with 10 per cent. These proportions have not changed over at least seven years. [31a]

▮ There are big differences in the proportion of households possessing contents insurance, depending on their income and tenure. In particular, almost half of families living in council flats lack such insurance, compared with less than 10 per cent of home owners. [31b]

Other key points and relevant research

▮ People living in rural areas are among those least likely to make use of demand-led information and leisure public services (including libraries, museums and sports/leisure facilities). While people in high income areas, middle income areas and low income areas had used these services on average between 15 and 17 times a year, the figure for country dwellers was only 13.[35]

▮ One outcome of retail exclusion is the relationship between the likelihood of having a healthy diet and deprivation. While other factors contribute, inequalities in access to good quality retail facilities is at least a partial explanation for the fact that 32 per cent of men in the most deprived areas[36] eat fresh fruit every day, compared with 55 per cent in the least deprived areas.[37]

▮ In view of the problems with transport provision in rural areas, car ownership is often seen to be a necessity for access to employment and services.[38] However, car ownership is far from universal in rural areas. In accessible, remote and very remote rural areas, around 20 per cent of households do not have access to a car. The same proportion do not possess a driving licence.[39]

▮ An aspect of financial exclusion is the disparity across neighbourhood types in the level of savings and investments. In 1999, sixty-five per cent of people living in areas defined as 'disadvantaged council estates – deprived schemes' were without any assets, compared with only 15 per cent in high income areas. There is also marked variation in the ownership of assets: thus, whereas more than 50 per cent of people in Glasgow and North Lanarkshire have no savings, the figure for the Grampian region is only 30 per cent.[40]

▮ The proportion of households without bank or building society accounts is higher in Scotland than in Great Britain as a whole. This is the case for both households in the poorest fifth of the income distribution (30 per cent compared with 19 per cent) and households with average incomes (9 per cent compared with 5 per cent).[41]

Satisfaction with services

Indicator 29

Around a third of people from manual backgrounds are dissatisfied with the quality of services provided by their council.

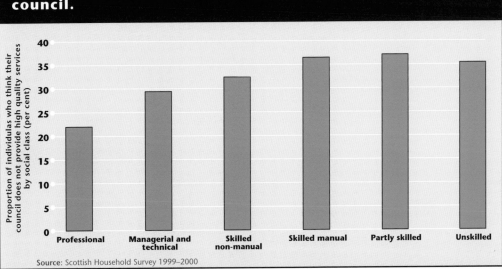

Source: Scottish Household Survey 1999–2000

Those living in accessible rural and remote rural locations are more likely to find certain services inconvenient than those living in other areas.

Source: Scottish Household Survey 1999–2000

The first graph shows the proportion of residents who think council services are not of high quality. This is defined as those who 'tend to disagree' or 'strongly disagree' with the question 'Do you agree/disagree that council provides high quality services?' This graph is based on the responses of approximately 60 per cent of the sample (just over 17,000 records). This is because data for this question is not available for all respondents using social class. But this does not significantly affect the results. Thirty-one per cent of the population in *total* (analysed without social class breakdowns) think services are not of a high quality, compared with 33 per cent when analysed *with* social class breakdowns.

The second graph shows levels of inconvenience for three services: doctors, post offices and grocery/food shops. It includes all who found the services 'fairly inconvenient' or 'very inconvenient'. The data is split by area type (urban to rural). See Indicator 27 for further details.

Note that for both graphs those categorised as 'Inadequately described and not stated' are not represented in the graphs but have been used to derive the figures. Data for both graphs is from the Scottish Household Survey for 1999 and 2000 together.

Overall adequacy of the indicator: **medium.** *The Scottish Household Survey is a large representative survey (see Indicator 1 for more details). But the smaller sample size in this indicator means it is not as robust as SHS data would otherwise allow.*

Satisfaction with public transport

Indicator 30

Half the people living in remote rural areas find public transport inconvenient compared with a tenth of those living in the four cities.

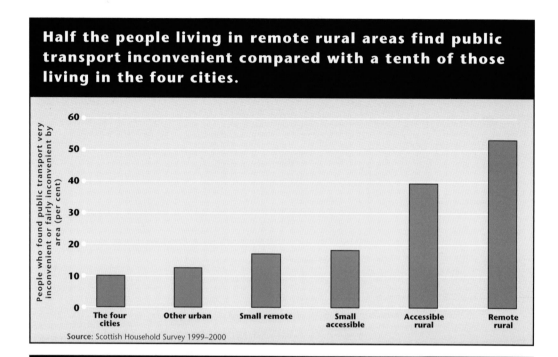

Source: Scottish Household Survey 1999–2000

Among those who cannot use public transport to go to work or school, people living in the country say it does not come often enough, whereas people living in towns say it takes too long.

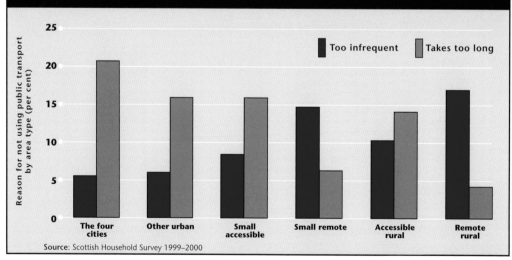

Source: Scottish Household Survey 1999–2000

The first graph shows people's perceptions of the convenience of public transport broken down by area type (urban-to-rural classification, see Indicator 27 for more details). For each of the area types, it shows the proportion that found public transport either 'very inconvenient' or 'fairly inconvenient'.

For those that replied it was not possible for them to use public transport (those who answered 'no' to the question 'Would it be possible for you to use public transport for the journey to and from work/school/college/university?'), the second graph shows the proportions citing two particular reasons, where the proportions differ significantly between area types. Note that these two reasons were selected from a wider selection, of which the most commonly cited for each area type was 'inconvenient'.

The data source in both cases is the Scottish Household Survey, combining data for the years 1999 and 2000.

Overall adequacy of the indicator: **high**. *The Scottish Household Survey is a large government survey (including approximately 31,000 households over two years) designed to be representative of private households and of the adult population in private households in Scotland.*

Without a bank or building society account

Indicator 31

A third of the poorest households do not have any type of bank/building society account, compared with a tenth of households on average incomes.

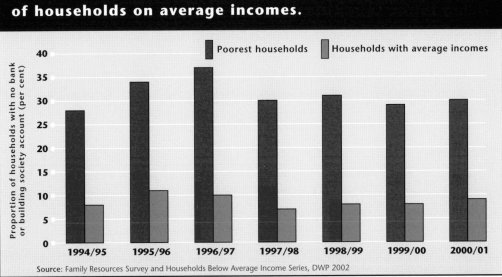

Legend: ■ Poorest households ■ Households with average incomes

Y-axis: Proportion of households with no bank or building society account (per cent)

X-axis: 1994/95, 1995/96, 1996/97, 1997/98, 1998/99, 1999/00, 2000/01

Source: Family Resources Survey and Households Below Average Income Series, DWP 2002

Half of all families living in council flats do not have home contents insurance, compared with 1 in 10 of home owners.

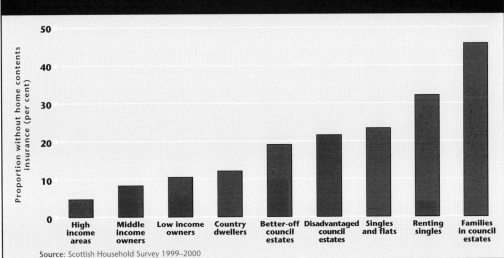

Y-axis: Proportion without home contents insurance (per cent)

X-axis: High income areas, Middle income owners, Low income owners, Country dwellers, Better-off council estates, Disadvantaged council estates, Singles and flats, Renting singles, Families in council estates

Source: Scottish Household Survey 1999–2000

The first graph shows the percentage of households without any kind of bank, building society or any other kind of account with separate figures for households in the poorest fifth of the income distribution and for households on average (middle fifth of the income distribution). Income is household disposable income equivalised, and is measured before housing costs. Note that although the statistics are for Scottish households only, the allocations to income quintile are those for the total GB population income distribution. Data is for 1994/95 to 2000/01, the earliest and latest the data is available for respectively.

Data is taken from the Family Resources Survey (FRS) and the Households Below Average Income.

The second graph shows households without home contents insurance broken down by mosaic type. The data is from the Scottish Household Survey, combining data for the years 1999 and 2000.

*Overall adequacy of the indicator: **medium**. The FRS is probably the most representative of the surveys that gather information on the extent to which people have bank and other types of account. However, care should be taken when looking at change over time because sampling variation for individual years is can be large in relation to the changes over time.*

Community

This section touches on a number of issues relating to 'community' in two senses of that word: first, as the local area in which people live and, second, as the organisations and institutions that make up society.

Crime and fear of crime have for some years now been recognised as issues of particular importance within deprived neighbourhoods, this importance being reflected in the standing the subject is given in official reports. The Scottish Executive's Social Justice Report, for example, includes two relevant measures, namely reducing the fear of crime among elderly people and reducing crime rates in disadvantaged areas. Crime in turn sits at the centre of a broader range of concerns to do with antisocial behaviour more generally.

To leave it at this, though, is not only to create a very one sided-picture but also to encourage a one-sided approach to the subject of how to 'improve' local areas. What it leaves out of account are the kind of things that communities may want *more* of, as well as what they want less of. A sense of this can be gleaned from a recent community-based study in the West Lothian village of Addiewell, where the provision of space and facilities within the village, especially for children and young people, was one of the subjects identified as being important. More specifically, the study mentioned activities for young people within the community centre, opportunities in the village for recreation such as fishing and cycling, and the re-location of swings in safe and dry areas.

The Addiewell study also highlighted other points that would help foster a sense of community, including: a focal point for people to meet; opportunities for social integration; the extent of participation by local people in community meetings and the like; and the importance of communication with, and participation by, the council. The fact that matters to do with the good functioning of the community came up in a study whose overall focus was health improvement is testimony to the fact that they were perceived by people to bring wider benefits and enhance general well-being, rather than just being important in their own right.

This chimes with the 'academic' view that community participation, as an element of 'social capital',[42] can contribute to economic success, sustainable development and the reduction of poverty. Communities with higher levels of social involvement and trust, it is argued, are more likely to secure responsive, efficient services from local government and to have the capacity to improve their general circumstances. Scotland is seen as having a well-developed civic leadership and capacity to mobilise to assert the needs of the poor and those excluded from the mainstream.[43]

Once again, though, the question is whether involvement and trust are evenly distributed across Scotland's communities or whether, in fact, what could be called community participation is weakest in areas where arguably it is needed most, namely those which are most deprived.

Topics, map and indicators

The three indicators and map in this section cover two aspects of this subject, namely:

I Attitudes towards the local area.

I Participation.

In spite of a desire to do otherwise, it has not been possible to produce a balanced set of indicators of *attitudes towards the local area*: our indicators are robustly negative. The first [32a] illustrates **the principal reasons why people dislike their local area**, with the results broken down by socio-economic group. It is supported by an indicator [32b] which shows the **proportion of people who feel very unsafe walking alone in their area at night**, with the results broken down this time by social class. This is a proxy measure for the uneven distribution of criminal activity (or perception of criminal activity) according to the level of deprivation of an area.

The first indicator connected with *participation* in the community measures **the proportion of people who feel involved in their local community** [33a], with the results broken down into the six category 'urban–rural hierarchy', from the four cities to remote rural areas. This is supported by an indicator [33b] which measures **the proportion of people helping a charity or other organisation on an unpaid basis in the last year**, with the results broken down according to the respondents' occupation. This graph highlights disparities in the extent of community involvement by a proxy for the level of deprivation of an area.

The second of the *participation* indicators [34b] and its accompanying map [Map F] measure **the percentage turnout by parliamentary constituency in the 2001 General Election**. The indicator shows the nine constituencies with the lowest turnout, the nine with the next lowest turnout, the next 18 and the remaining 36.

The other graph for this indicator [34a] draws on the same data to show **the change in the percentage turnout between 1997 and 2001 according to the level of the turnout in 1997**, with the results shown for four equal groups of constituencies, namely the 18 with the lowest turnout in 1997, the 18 with the next lowest, and so on. [44]

What the indicators show

I People from manual, partly skilled and unskilled backgrounds are more than twice as likely to dislike their neighbourhood because of young people 'hanging around' or vandalism compared with those from professional or managerial occupations. [32a]

I There are also marked differences in the proportion of people (of all ages) who report feeling very unsafe walking alone in their area at night. Although the proportion overall is low (around 10 per cent) only 4 per cent of those from professional and managerial backgrounds report this problem, compared with 20 per cent among those from unskilled backgrounds. [32b]

I The extent to which people feel involved with their community is higher the smaller the community is, and the more remote its location: around 1 in 5 in urban areas, but upward of 1 in 3 in rural ones. Nevertheless, the norm, even in rural areas, is for people not to feel involved; and in urban areas, this is the sense of the vast majority. [33a]

▮ Devoting time to helping a charity or other organisation is an activity far more associated with people from professional and managerial backgrounds – more than 2 in 5 – than those from unskilled backgrounds – fewer than 1 in 5. [33b]

▮ The problem of low turnout in elections is overwhelmingly associated with Glasgow, with 8 out of 9 of the constituencies with the lowest turnout being in Glasgow (Edinburgh Central being the other one). Turnout within this lowest group ranged from just under 40 per cent (Glasgow Shettleston) to 52 per cent (Edinburgh Central). By contrast, two-thirds of seats (48) recorded turnouts between 55 per cent and 65 per cent. [Map F and 34b]

▮ The fall in turnout between 1997 and 2001 varied between 14 percentage points across the 18 constituencies with the lowest 1997 turnouts, and 12½ percentage points in the 18 with the highest. Expressing these falls in proportion to the 1997 turnout, these differences appear larger. Thus in the 18 constituencies with the lowest turnout in 1997, twenty-two per cent of those who voted then did not do so in 2001; in the 18 with the highest turnout, by contrast, only 16½ per cent failed to vote in 2001. [34a]

Other key points and relevant research

▮ Analysis of the Scottish Household Survey suggests that, among those responsible for children, people from manual backgrounds are more dissatisfied than those from non-manual backgrounds with parks and sports facilities. The differences are, however, slight and the overall level of dissatisfaction is on average around 1 in 8.

▮ The proportion of people who perceive crime to be an extremely serious problem fell quite sharply over the 1990s, from around 1 in 2 in 1992, to around 1 in 4 in 1999. However, people from manual backgrounds continue to be more likely than people from non-manual backgrounds to regard crime as extremely serious: for example, 32 per cent and 23 per cent respectively in 1999.[45]

▮ The Scottish Crime Survey shows that feeling very unsafe walking alone at night is far more of a problem for women than men, and more for those aged over 60 than those under. So, on average, 3½ per cent of men but 16 per cent of women report feeling very unsafe. For those over 60, however, the proportions rise to 6 per cent and 23 per cent respectively.[46]

▮ The Scottish Crime Survey 1999 shows that residents from the poorest council estates were the group most likely to perceive crime as 'very common' in their area.[47]

▮ Analysis of the Scottish Household Survey shows a marked urban–rural split in volunteering in the local community. While 22 per cent of adults in the 'four cities' had volunteered their time in 2000, twenty-four per cent of those in 'other urban' areas had done so, whereas 41 per cent of those in 'remote rural' areas and 39 per cent in 'very remote rural' areas had participated in voluntary activities.[48]

▮ Both age and gender have an impact on the probability of volunteering. Women are slightly more likely to give up their time as volunteers, and the age group most inclined to volunteer is 35 to 59.[49]

❚ Looked at nationally, turnout in parliamentary elections in Scotland fluctuated between 70 and 80 per cent between 1955 and 1997. The 2001 turnout of 58 per cent therefore marked a huge change. The real break, however, occurred with the election for the Scottish Parliament in 1999, with a turnout of 59 per cent.[50]

Satisfaction with local area

Indicator 32

People from both skilled and unskilled occupations are much more likely to dislike their neighbourhood because of young people 'hanging around' or vandalism, compared with those from professional occupations.

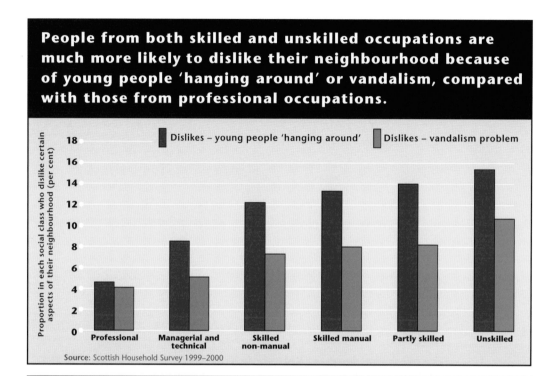

Source: Scottish Household Survey 1999–2000

People from manual backgrounds are much more likely to feel very unsafe after dark in their local area tha n people from non-manual backgrounds.

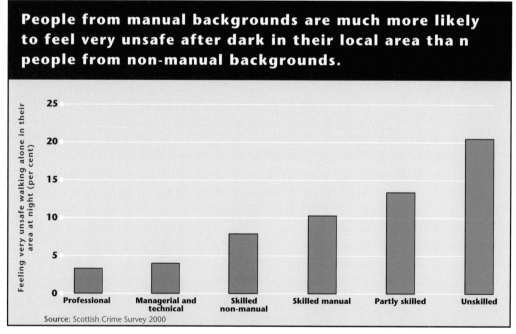

Source: Scottish Crime Survey 2000

The first graph shows the proportion of people who dislike their neighbourhood because of young people hanging around or vandalism. These two reasons were selected from a wider list because they were the top two reasons given. The data is split by social class. The data source is the Scottish Household Survey, combining data for 1999 and 2000.

Note that this graph is based on the responses of approximately 60 per cent of the sample in the survey (just over 17,000 records). This is because the data for this question is not available for all respondents when analysed using social class. To compare the reliability of these results with the full sample, analysis was carried out without social class. The proportion of the population in total who dislike their neighbourhood because of young people hanging around and vandalism is 12 per cent and 8 per cent respectively. This compares with 11 per cent and 7 per cent when analysed with social class.

The second graph shows the extent to which people felt 'very unsafe' walking alone in their area after dark. The data is split to show how levels differ by social class. The data is taken from the 2000 Scottish Crime Survey.

*Overall adequacy of the indicator: **high**. The Scottish Household Survey is a large representative survey (see Indicator 1 for more details). The second graph can be considered high. The Scottish Crime Survey is a well-established survey. Due to the structure of the questions, we can be fairly confident that the measure is a good indicator of attitudes towards walking alone 'after dark' rather than other generalist attitudes or anxiety.*

Participation in the community

A fifth of those living in urban areas felt involved in their local community. This a much smaller proportion than in rural areas.

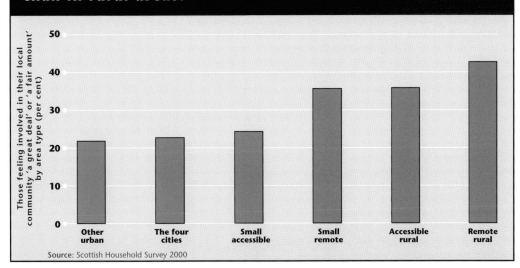

Source: Scottish Household Survey 2000

People from manual backgrounds, especially the unskilled, are much less likely to have helped a charity or organisation than people from managerial or professional backgrounds.

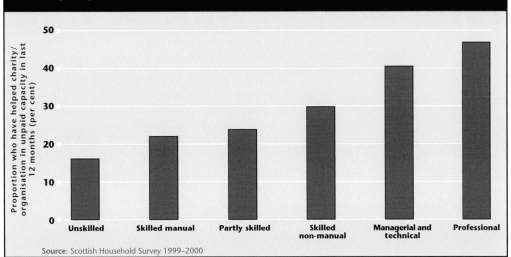

Source: Scottish Household Survey 1999–2000

The first graph measures the extent to which people feel involved with their local community. It includes all those who felt involved 'a fair amount' or a 'great deal' when asked 'How involved do you feel in your local community?' The data is split by area type (urban to rural, see Indicator 27 for more details).

The second graph measures the extent to which people took part in volunteering. It includes those that helped charity or an organisation in an unpaid capacity in last 12 months. The data is split by social class.

The data source in both cases is the Scottish Household Survey 2000. Note that the second graph is based on the responses of approximately 55 per cent of the sample in the Scottish Household Survey for the year 2000 (just over 8,000 records). This is because the data for this question is not available for all respondents when analysed using social class. To compare the reliability of these results with the full sample analysis was carried out without social class breakdowns. The proportion of the population in total who helped a charity or organisation was 26 per cent. This compares with 30 per cent when analysed with social class breakdowns.

Overall adequacy of the indicator: **high**. *The Scottish Household Survey is a large representative survey (see Indicator 1 for more details). The second graph can be regarded as low as it is based on a much smaller sample size.*

MAP F: The percentage turnout across Scottish constituencies in the 2001 General Election ranged from 40 per cent to 70 per cent.

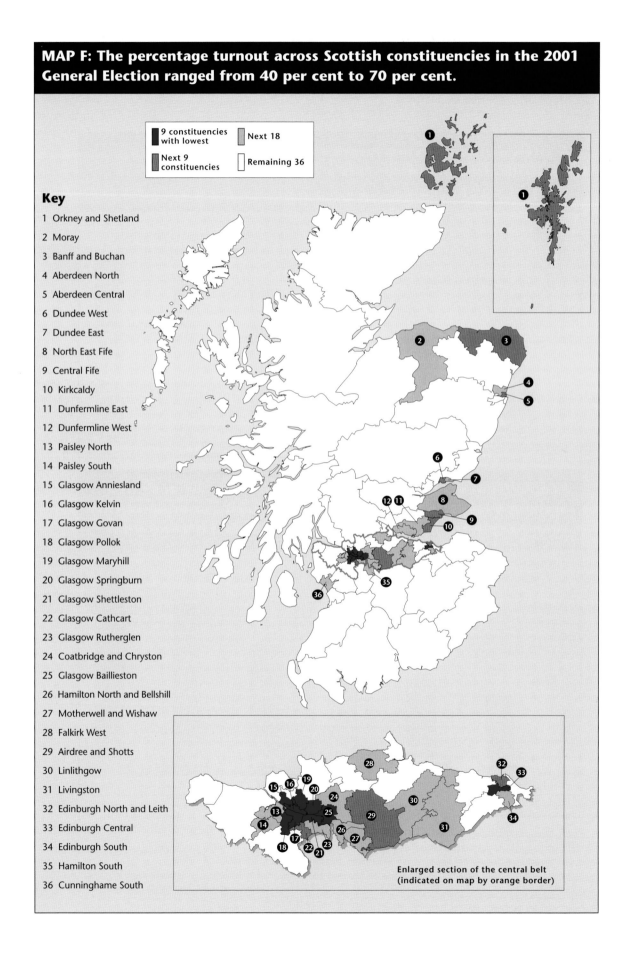

9 constituencies with lowest

Next 9 constituencies

Next 18

Remaining 36

Key

1 Orkney and Shetland

2 Moray

3 Banff and Buchan

4 Aberdeen North

5 Aberdeen Central

6 Dundee West

7 Dundee East

8 North East Fife

9 Central Fife

10 Kirkcaldy

11 Dunfermline East

12 Dunfermline West

13 Paisley North

14 Paisley South

15 Glasgow Anniesland

16 Glasgow Kelvin

17 Glasgow Govan

18 Glasgow Pollok

19 Glasgow Maryhill

20 Glasgow Springburn

21 Glasgow Shettleston

22 Glasgow Cathcart

23 Glasgow Rutherglen

24 Coatbridge and Chryston

25 Glasgow Baillieston

26 Hamilton North and Bellshill

27 Motherwell and Wishaw

28 Falkirk West

29 Airdree and Shotts

30 Linlithgow

31 Livingston

32 Edinburgh North and Leith

33 Edinburgh Central

34 Edinburgh South

35 Hamilton South

36 Cunninghame South

Enlarged section of the central belt (indicated on map by orange border)

Voting

Indicator
34

Compared with 1997, the turnout in the 2001 General Election fell proportionally the furthest in those constituencies where it was already the lowest.

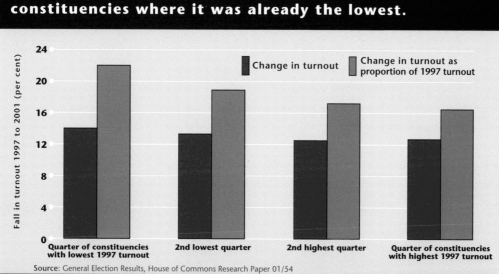

Source: General Election Results, House of Commons Research Paper 01/54

The percentage turnout across Scottish constituencies in the 2001 General Election ranged from 40 to 70 per cent.

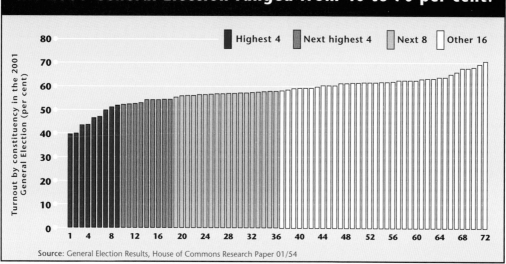

Source: General Election Results, House of Commons Research Paper 01/54

The first graph shows the change in turnout at the 2001 General Election compared with the 1997 General Election. The data is split into quarters showing the constituencies with the lowest to the highest turnout in 1997. The data source is the House of Commons.

The second graph which accompanies the map, shows the distribution of turnout at the 2001 general election by constituency. The data source is the House of Commons.

Overall adequacy of the indicator: **high.** *Data is based on an administrative count of actual votes in all constituencies and is thought to be reliable.*

Commentary

Community perceptions of well-being

Peter Kelly, Poverty Alliance

Over the last few years the notion of community well-being has become very important to the government's plans for community regeneration. This notion is one that is far from well defined, however, and consequently is very difficult to measure. Even with a clear notion of 'well-being', it may remain difficult to relate this to what communities understand well-being to mean. This is an important issue for politicians and policy makers, for if the programmes they develop to improve the well-being of individuals and communities do not reflect the priorities of those communities then there will be little improvement in well-being. It is therefore about far more than simply measuring the change in certain key indicators. It is also about ensuring genuine community participation in the development of policies and indicators to tackle poverty and social exclusion.

Concepts of well-being draw heavily on studies of individual and community health and definitions of quality of life. Just as the health and quality of life of an individual is the outcome of a range of complex factors, so too will the general well-being of a community be dependent on similar factors.

This complexity has been acknowledged in the Community Planning structures that are currently emerging in Scotland. Councils in Scotland will have a new statutory duty to promote and improve the well-being of the people and areas they are responsible for. This is as a result of the Local Government in Scotland (2002) Bill that is currently progressing through Parliament. This will also place upon Local Authorities the statutory responsibility to produce Community Plans in partnership with a range of other local agencies. This requirement recognises the complexity involved in improving the well-being of a community. Community plans should be prepared in consultation with local people and with other local agencies that have a contribution to make to well-being. In this way Community Planning should recognise the interrelatedness of economic, social and environmental well-being. The new power also gives councils more scope to act, to take whatever actions they believe will promote the well-being of the community.

Community planning structures represent an important opportunity to promote the well-being of communities in an innovative and comprehensive way. However, the vagueness of the concept also presents problems in defining what policy measures will actually promote the well-being of communities. Economic, social and environmental well-being covers the range of activities of national and local government, health trusts, the voluntary and private sectors and other organisations. Indeed, the Community Planning Taskforce has identified more than 250 indicators relating to the Scottish Executive's agenda's on social justice, economic development, health, education and the environment.[51]

Taken together, these indicators provide an almost overwhelming amount of information on the 'well-being' of communities. However, these indicators are driven by the policy agenda that the Scottish Executive has set. As such, one could argue that they are in fact better indicators of how well any particular policy initiative is progressing. Whilst these indicators may well give an account of community well-being it is not true therefore to say that they provide us with community perceptions of well-being. To do this would require the use of indicators developed by the community themselves.

Research carried out in Addiewell, West Lothian, has attempted to develop community based health indicators using participatory approaches. In this study local residents were interviewed, and indicators developed from these interviews which were validated by focus groups. The indicators were focused around six issues: transport, health and social services, environment, housing, facilities for young people and sense of community.

The indicators developed in this project differed from those used in public health generally. Although the project was aimed at developing indicators of health, the indicators focused more on 'life circumstances' and were perhaps broader than those that would be used by health professionals. The measures used to monitor change in the indicators were often closely related to local concerns. However, the authors of the report felt that the indicators that were developed could be generalisable to other policy areas. Indeed, it was felt that the process of developing community generated indicators has an important role to play in understanding the impact and effectiveness of policies at a local level.

Including community generated indicators in the monitoring of poverty and social exclusion will not be an easy process. Such indicators may not always be easily quantifiable or fit neatly into existing social inclusion policies. This is the challenge for those whose task it is to develop and monitor the implementation of the Scottish Executive's social inclusion policies. More structured, formalised arrangements are needed for communities to engage in the process of monitoring social inclusion policies in Scotland. Without such arrangements the engagement of those who experience poverty and social exclusion will not become a reality, and without this engagement the Executive will fail effectively to monitor the impact that their policies have on people's lives.

Summary

Homeless households

The number of households assessed as homeless or potentially homeless rose by 50 per cent during the 1990s. Households in rented accommodation are one-and-a-half times more likely to be overcrowded than those who are buying their home with a mortgage.

Affordable housing

The annual number of new lets by public authorities remained in the 40,000s during the 1990s, although the total stock of public housing declined by more than a third. Social rented accommodation is a smaller proportion of the housing stock in rural areas than urban areas.

Households without central heating

Households with a low income are more likely than average to lack central heating, but the numbers have been coming down sharply. Those living in rented flats are much less likely to have central heating than those living in houses they own or are buying with a mortgage.

Satisfaction with services

Around a third of people from manual backgrounds are dissatisfied with the quality of services provided by their council. Those living in accessible rural and remote rural locations are more likely to find certain services inconvenient than those living in other areas.

Satisfaction with public transport

Half the people living in remote rural areas find public transport inconvenient compared with a tenth of those living in the four cities. Among those who cannot use public transport to go to work or school, people in the country say it does not come often enough, whereas people in the town say it takes too long.

Without a bank or building society account

A third of the poorest households do not have any type of bank/building society account compared with a tenth of households on average incomes. Half of all families living in council flats do not have home contents insurance, compared with 1 in 10 of home owners.

Satisfaction with local area

People from both skilled and unskilled occupations are much more likely to dislike their neighbourhood because of young people 'hanging around' or vandalism, compared with those from professional occupations. People from manual backgrounds are much more likely to feel unsafe at night in their local area than people from non-manual backgrounds.

Participation in the community

A fifth of those living in urban areas feel involved in their local community. This is a much smaller proportion than in rural areas. People from manual backgrounds, especially the unskilled, are much less likely to have helped a charity or organisation than people from managerial or professional backgrounds.

Voting

Compared with 1997, turnout in the 2001 General Election fell proportionally the furthest in those constituencies where it was lowest to start with. The percentage turnout across Scottish constituencies in the 2001 General Election ranged from 40 per cent to 70 per cent.

Policy summaries

Selected major initiatives under way

Scottish Social Justice Annual Report milestones

Chapter	Relevant Scottish Social Justice Annual Report (SJAR) Milestones
Poverty and low income	1 Reducing the proportion of our children living in workless households. 2 Reducing the proportion of children living in low income households. 4 All of our children will have access to quality care and early learning before entering school. 14 Reducing the proportion of working age people with low incomes. 19 Reducing the proportion of older people with low incomes. 20 Increasing the proportion of working age people contributing to a non-state pension.
Employment and education	3 Increasing the proportion of our children who attain the appropriate levels in reading, writing and maths by the end of Primary 2 and Primary 7. 7 Halving the proportion of 16- to 19-year-olds who are not in education, training or employment. 8 All of our young people leaving local authority care will have achieved at least English and Maths Standard Grades and have access to appropriate housing options. 9 Bringing the poorest performing 20 per cent of pupils, in terms of Standard Grades achievement, closer to the performance of all pupils. 10 Reducing by a third the days lost every year through exclusion from school and truancy. 13 Reducing the proportion of unemployed working age people. 15 Increasing the employment rates of disadvantaged groups, such as lone parents and ethnic minorities, that are relatively disadvantaged in the labour market. 16 Increasing the proportion of students from under-represented, disadvantaged groups and areas in higher education compared with the overall student population in higher education. 24 Reducing the gap in unemployment rates between the worst areas and the average rate for Scotland.
Ill health	5 Improving the well-being of our young children through reductions in the proportion of women smoking during pregnancy, the percentage of low birth-weight babies, dental decay among 5-year-olds and increasing the proportion of women breastfeeding. 11 Improving the health of young people through reductions in smoking by 12- to 15-year-olds, teenage pregnancies among 13- to 15-year-olds, and the rate of suicides among young people. 18 Improving the health of families by reducing smoking, alcohol misuse, poor diet and mortality rates from coronary heart disease. 22 Increasing the number of older people taking exercise and reducing the rates of mortality from coronary heart disease and the prevalence of respiratory disease. 25 Reducing the incidence of drug misuse in general and of injecting and sharing of needles in particular.
Quality of life and social cohesion	6 Reducing the number of households with children living in temporary accommodation. 8 All of our young people leaving local authority care will have achieved at least English and Maths Standard Grades and have access to appropriate housing options. 12 No one has to sleep rough. 17 Increasing the proportion of people with learning disabilities able to live at home or in a 'homely' environment. 21 Increasing the proportion of older people able to live independently by doubling the proportion of older people receiving respite care at home and increasing home care opportunities. 23 Reducing the fear of crime among older people. 26 Reducing crime rates in disadvantaged areas. 27 Increasing the quality and variety of homes in our most disadvantaged communities. 28 Increasing the number of people from across all communities taking part in voluntary activities.

Poverty and low income

Policy	Government	Start year	Budget/target/comments
National Minimum Wage	UK	1999	When first introduced, set at £3.60 for those over 22 years, unless in an exempt category or on a registered training scheme (in which case only £3.20). £3.00 per hour for those aged 18 to 21. Uprated each year and now £4.20 (and £3.60).
Pensioners' Minimum Income Guarantee	UK	1999	When introduced, set at £75 a week for single pensioners and £116.60 for pensioner couples, representing increases of around £4 and £7 respectively over the levels of Income Support that were previously available. Uprated each year and now £98.15 and £149.80 respectively. To be replaced by the Pension Credit in April 2003.
Second State Pension	UK	2002	An extension to SERPS and will double income provided by SERPS for those on incomes of less than £10,800.
Increase in Child Benefit	UK	1999	Increased in April 1999 to £14.40 for eldest child (a £2.50 increase above inflation) and now £15.75 for eldest child, £10.55 for other children and £17.55 for eldest child of lone parent.
Increase in Child Allowance within Income Support	UK	1998	Uprated each year. Child premium to be replaced by the Child Tax Credit in April 2003.
Working Families Tax Credit (replaced Family Credit)	UK	1999	For families/lone parents with one child or more, who are working for a minimum of 16 hours per week. It consists of a basic element, an element for those working 30+ hours per week, and an element for each child. Help towards childcare cost is also available. When first introduced, guaranteed a weekly gross income of £200 for a family with one full-time worker and with no tax until £235 per week for families with one full-timer (55p taper, down from 70p under Family Credit). Uprated each year and now £225. Estimated to have helped 114,000 families in Scotland. To be replaced by a combination of Working Tax Credit and Child Tax Credit in April 2003.
Childcare allowance (part of the Working Families Tax Credit)	UK	1999	When first introduced, up to 70 per cent of childcare costs for working parents, up to a limit of £100 for one child and £150 for 2+ children. Now £135 for one child and £200 for 2+ children.
Disabled Person's Tax Credit (replaced Disability Working Allowance)	UK	1999	Originally guaranteed a weekly income of £231 for a couple with one child. Uprated each year and now £264 per week. Operates like the Working Families Tax Credit, except no children are required to be eligible. To be replaced by Working Tax Credit in April 2003.
Children's Tax Credit (replaced Married Couple's Allowance)	UK	2001	Payable to anyone paying tax who has a child aged 16 or under (implemented as a reduction in the tax bill of the claimant). Maximum tax reduction of £529 per annum (double in the first year of the child's life). This compares with £197 for the Married Couple's Allowance. Maximum amount for the family element will be given to those on an annual income of £32,750 or less. For every £15 above this, £1 will be deducted. Worth up to £520 per year for around 400,000 Scottish families.

	Government	Start year	Budget/target/comments
'Baby Tax Credit'	UK	2002	Allows lone parents on Income Support to keep up to £10 per week of their child maintenance.
Winter Fuel Payments	UK	1997/98	Eligible households received £100 in 1999/2000 and £200 in 2000/01, 2001/02, and 2002/03. All pensioners in receipt of the State Retirement Pension or a social security benefit (excluding Child, Housing and Council Tax Benefits) are eligible.
Working group 'Partnerships Against Poverty'	Scotland and UK		Objective is to evaluate existing work and consider new initiatives on take-up of social security benefits paid to older people.
Changing Children Services Fund	Scotland	2002	£82 million 2001–04. A joint initiative to provide better-integrated services for children.
Sure Start Scotland	Scotland	1999	£42 million from 1999 to 2002 (for 5,000 children) and £19 million per year 2002 to 2004. Aims to provide support for families with very young children to ensure that children are in a position to take full advantage of subsequent opportunities, including most immediately pre-school education.

Employment and education
Education

Policy	Government	Start year	Budget/target/comments
Beattie Inclusiveness Projects	Scotland	1998	£23 million in 2001 to 2004. Aims to help young people make the transition to post-school education.
Early Intervention Initiative	Scotland	1999	£60 million in 1999 to 2004. Supports a range of projects aiming to help children at the early stages of primary school who have difficulty in the basic skills of reading, writing and numeracy.
New Community Schools	Scotland	1999	£37 million in 2001 for 62 pilot projects involving 400 schools. Aims to promote social inclusion and raise educational standards through partnership working.
Education Maintenance Allowance	Scotland	1999	£9 million in 2002 to 2004. Allowance is payable to young people aged 16 to 19 from low-income households, to encourage them to stay on in education beyond the age of 16.
Learndirect Scotland	Scotland	2000	£17 million in 2002 to 2004. Provides a free telephone helpline which gives out information and advice on learning opportunities in Scotland. Achieved its target of creating a network of 300 learning centres by the end of March 2002.
Adult Literacy and Numeracy	Scotland	2001	£23 million in 2001 to 2004, of which £19 million will be routed through local authorities to Community Learning Strategy Partnerships. Targets include the doubling of annual capacity to help 34,000 people each year by 2004; and helping 80,000 people in total to improve their literacy and numeracy by 2004.

	Government	Start year	Budget/target/comments
Discipline Task Group	Scotland	2001	Remit includes examining ways to involve parents further in motivating and supporting their children and to foster positive attitudes towards education.
Enterprise education	Scotland	2001	Focused on 5- to 14-year-olds in 2,300 primary and 400 secondary schools. £5 million in 2001 to 2004.
Lone Parents into Higher/Further Education	Scotland	2001	£24 million. Key elements include £1,000 grants to pay for formal childcare for lone parents in full-time education, £7 million for further education colleges to widen childcare provision to meet locally identified needs, and £8 million to allow local authorities to support out-of-school clubs in disadvantaged areas.
Community Learning Strategy Partnerships	Scotland	2002	An extra £19 million in 2002 to 2004. Aims to create new opportunities for those seeking help with literacy and numeracy through partnerships between public, voluntary and community-based organisations.

Employment

Policy	Government	Start year	Budget/target/comments
Enterprise Networks	Scotland		Scottish Enterprise comprises Scottish Enterprise National (SEN) and 12 Local Enterprise Companies (LECs). In 1999/2000, total Scottish Enterprise spend was £460 million. Aims include creating innovative and far-sighted organisations; encouraging learning and enterprise; creating an inclusive society and developing a competitive place. Provides support for new companies and delivers training programmes.
Beattie Inclusiveness Projects	Scotland	1998	£23 million in 2001 to 2004. Aims to help young people make the transition to training and employment.
New Futures Fund	Scotland	1998	£15 million in 2002 to 2005. Assistance for young people experiencing difficulties entering the job market. Such disadvantage includes disability, homelessness and drug misuse.
Future Skills Scotland	Scotland	2001	Aims to provide improved projections of local employment needs and better matching of people to jobs by improving the planning of education and training needs and working with employers to help them adjust their employment and training policies to meet future trends.
Careers Scotland	Scotland	2002	Aims to operate as a one-stop shop for careers guidance services, assisting customers with job vacancies, learning and training opportunities. Also aims to improve the employability and enterprise skills of people, increasing participation in learning and employment and acting as the leading national advocate for the guidance and employability sector.

Policy	Government	Start year	Budget/target/comments
New Deal for the long-term unemployed	UK	1998	Aims to move people unemployed for two years or more into work.
New Deal for Disabled People	UK	1998	Aims to move disabled people into work.
New Deal for Lone Parents	UK	1997	Aims to achieve an overall 70 per cent employment for lone parents by 2010. 20,000 have participated in the programme in Scotland, with 9,000 finding work and 1,000 now on a training or education course.
New Deal for 18- to 24- year-olds	UK	1998	Aims to move young adults into work. 35,000 young Scots have secured jobs through the New Deal.
New Deal for the over-50s	UK	1999	Aimed to move over-50s into voluntary work. Includes payments of tax-free employment credit, a training grant, and support and advice.
New Deal for partners of unemployed people	UK	1999	Aimed to move eligible people into work.
Childcare Strategy	Scotland	1998	Aims to create more accessible and affordable new childcare places for children aged 0 to 14 in every neighbourhood, including both formal childcare and support for informal arrangements.

III health
Birth, death and disability

Policy	Government	Start year	Budget/target/comments
Scottish Community Diet Project	Scotland	1996	Aims to improve Scotland's diet and health, and the inequalities that exist within both, by increasing the effectiveness of those working within and with Scotland's low income communities to improve access to and take-up of a healthy, varied, balanced diet. Offers grants of between £500 and £3,000, available to anyone tackling the barriers to a healthy diet with and within Scotland's low-income communities as outlined in the Scottish Diet Action Plan.
Healthy Living Centres	Scotland	2000	Supported by £35 million from the New Opportunities Fund. Aim to improve the health and general well-being of the most disadvantaged members of the population. They support national strategies to improve health and reduce health inequalities.
Coronary Heart Disease and Stroke Strategy for Scotland	Scotland	2001	A national target of reducing the age standardised mortality rate from coronary heart disease in people under age 75 by 50 per cent between 1995 and 2010 (i.e. from 143 to 72 deaths per 100,000 population) was set in the White Paper Towards a Healthier Scotland.
Smoking in deprived areas	Scotland	2000	Involves expanding databases and networks of information on smoking initiatives.
Health Promoting Schools	Scotland	2002	A health promoting school is one in which all members of the school community work together to provide children and young people with integrated and positive experiences and structures, which promote and protect their health.

	Government	Start year	Budget/target/comments
Health Demonstration Projects	Scotland	2000	£15 million in 2000 to 2003 to fund four locally based projects are acting as a learning and teaching resource for the rest of Scotland. These projects cover such areas as child health, teenage health, heart disease and cancer screening.
Infant and Child Nutrition Strategy	Scotland	2000	Scottish Executive in partnership with the World Health Organisation. Aims to improve the health and survival rates of woman and their children by developing better feeding practices, in particular breastfeeding.

Young adults

Policy	Government	Start year	Budget/target/comments
Anti-Bullying Network	Scotland	2000	Includes a website, telephone information line, national conference, a programme encouraging local authorities to act, and network project workers who produce additional supporting materials to complement existing resources.
Mental Health and Well-Being Support Group	Scotland	2000	Aims to make sure that those employed by the NHS and local authorities are working together to provide the best services.
Suicide prevention policies	Scotland	2002	A pilot telephone helpline for people, particularly young men, who have feelings of depression or who may be at risk of suicide, with a long-term programme to tackle suicide and self-harm under consideration.
Scotland Against Drugs	Scotland	1996	£1½ million per year plus money raised from the private sector, of which £½ million goes to the Scottish Drugs Challenge Fund. Remit is to raise public awareness, and take a fresh approach to Scotland's growing drug misuse problem.
New Futures Fund	Scotland	1998	£15 million in 2002 to 2005. Targeted assistance for young people experiencing difficulties entering the job market, including those resulting from drug misuse.
Drugs strategy	Scotland	1999	£128 million.
Scottish Drug Enforcement Agency	Scotland	2000	£10 million 2001 to 2002. Targets for 2002/03 include increasing the number of arrests of persons involved in drug trafficking and other serious and organised crime by 5 per cent; increasing the weight of Class A drug seizures by 5 per cent; and increasing the number of criminal networks disrupted by 5 per cent.
Changing Children Services Fund	Scotland	2001	£82 million for 2001 to 2004, of which £18 million will be spent tackling drug abuse by or affecting young people.

Quality of life and social cohesion
Housing and homelessness

Policy	Government	Start year	Budget/target/comments
The Improvement and Repairs Grant System	Scotland	1970	Assists owners in the private sector to bring their homes up to the level of the Tolerable Standard and put them in a good state of repair or to make them wind and watertight.
Rough Sleepers Initiative (RSI)	Scotland	1997	£10 million per year until 2004. A Scottish Executive challenge fund intended to promote the development of facilities aimed at helping people who sleep rough into a more stable, settled life.
New Housing Partnership	Scotland	1997	£200 million plus £300 million of additional private sector investment for housing regeneration and development partnerships. Aims to provide 8,000 new and improved homes across Scotland.
Health and Homelessness Action Plan	Scotland	2001	Monitors the delivery of services to homeless people. NHS Boards' Action Plans will be for three years covering 2000–05 and must be delivered in partnership with local stakeholders.
Housing investment programme	Scotland	2001	£226 million in 2002/03. Aims to create decent and affordable housing for everyone in Scotland. Target is to fund the provision of 4,700 new and improved houses for rent and owner occupation in urban and rural areas, including provision for the homeless and those with particular housing needs.
Empty House Initiative	Scotland	1997	£7 million in 2001/02, the final year of the initiative. Assists local authorities, in partnership with others, to bring empty properties across all categories of ownership back into use.
Affordable Warmth Programme	Scotland	1999	A partnership programme (with Transco) to tackle fuel poverty through the provision of central heating, insulation and heating advice. Aims to benefit 100,000 houses over a five-year period.
Warm Deal	Scotland	1999	£15 million in 2002–04. Provides households dependent on benefit with a package of insulation measures up to a value of £500.
Supporting People	Scotland	2001	£15 million in 2001/02 to 2003/04. A new integrated policy and funding framework for housing support services. Aims to provide good quality services, focused on the needs of users, to enable vulnerable people to live independently in the community, in all types of accommodation and tenure.

	Government	Start year	Budget/target/comments
Central Heating Initiative	Scotland	2001	£70 million in 2002 to 2004. Aims to provide central heating in all council houses by April 2004, to all housing association tenants by 2004 and to all over-60s by March 2006.
National Mortgage to Rent Scheme	Scotland	2001	Target is to benefit around 70,000 households across all sectors of the stock. £1½ million in 2001/02. Aims to provide funding for Scottish homeowners in mortgage difficulty and to help families avoid repossession and to become tenants of their own homes.

Quality services

Policy	Government	Start year	Budget/target/comments
Scottish Rural Partnerships Fund	Scotland	1996	Aims to build community capacity in particular rural areas and meet to discuss and agree jointly the way forward to meet local needs within that area. Three elements: the Rural Challenge Fund, the Local Capital Grants Scheme, and the Rural Strategic Support Fund.
Wider Role Programme	Scotland	2000	£10 million in 2000–03. Provides funding for housing associations and co-operatives for non-housing activities such as employment, social amenities and crime prevention.
Modernising Government Fund	Scotland	2000	£26 million in 2000/01 to 2002 for 32 innovative public sector projects that were aimed at improving the quality, effectiveness and efficiency of public services.
Better Neighbourhood Services Fund	Scotland	2001	£90 million for 2001 to 2004. Aims to improve the provision of services in deprived areas through the support of pilot initiatives identified with communities.
Credit Union Action Plan	Scotland	2001	£1½ million. Credit unions can apply for one-off grants of £4,000 under the Credit Union Kickstart Fund.
Rural Transport Fund	Scotland	1998	£18 million 2001–04. Comprises the Rural Public Passenger Transport Fund, the Rural Community Transport Grant Scheme and the Rural Petrol Stations Grant Scheme.
Public Transport Fund	Scotland	1999	Provides funding for local authorities' local transport strategies to provide alternatives to car use, and to assist innovative investment in new railway stations, new bus lanes, new rapid transport systems and park and ride schemes.

Community

Policy	Government	Start year	Budget/target/comments
Local rural partnerships	Scotland	1996	54 in existence to improve the prospects for economic development in an area, to address issues relating to land use planning, to deliver local services in a way most geared to local needs, to improve local transport, and to encourage the most sustainable use of the natural resources of the area.
Initiative at the Edge	Scotland	1998	In particular communities, brings together the main government agencies in a way which encourages a strengthened, integrated approach to tackling the uncertainty facing fragile communities.
Social Inclusion Partnerships (SIPs)	Scotland	1999	£120 million in 2002–04, shared between 48 SIPs, of which 34 are comprehensive area-based initiatives, while the remaining 14 have a particular theme or focus. Aim to tackle the multiple problems associated with poverty and social exclusion in areas of greatest need and for socially excluded groups.
Reviving communities programme	Scotland	1999	£74 million in 2002/03. Part of the Communities Scotland Regeneration Plan. Aims to ensure that SIPs and others get the best out of existing community regeneration initiatives.
Empowering communities programme	Scotland	1999	£6 million in 2002/03. Part of the Communities Scotland Regeneration Plan. Aims to encourage community involvement in SIPs. Includes funding for the Coalfields Regeneration Trust.
Kickstart programme	Scotland	2000	£1/2 million in 2001–03. A capacity building initiative for local voluntary and community groups in relation to funding issues.
Working for Communities	Scotland	1999	Funding was provided for 13 Pathfinders, which were trying out new ways of delivering local services bringing them more in line with the wishes of people.
Communities First	Scotland	2002	£150 million in 2002–05. Aims to secure fairer shares of Lottery Funding for the most disadvantaged communities.
Scottish Centre for Regeneration	Scotland	2003	£3 million set aside for 2002–05. Works in partnership with other organisations to improve the quality and effectiveness of tackling deprivation.
Coalfields Regeneration Trust	UK	1999	£3 million in 2001/02 to 2003/04. Aims to help and support community initiatives in former mining communities.
Community Safety Partnerships	Scotland	1998	Funded by the Scottish Forum on Community Safety. Aims to improve crime prevention and community safety.
Active Communities Initiative	UK	1999	Aims to promote more positive attitudes to volunteering and community action and to increase the numbers and broaden the range of people getting involved in volunteering and community action.

References

Introduction

1   A particularly important difference is the fact of the Scottish Executive's *Social Justice Annual Report*. By contrast, the original *Monitoring Poverty and Social Exclusion* pre-dated not only that report, but also the UK government's equivalent, *Opportunity for All*.

2   For more information on this, see for instance Brown, U., Scott, G., Mooney, G., . Duncan, B., *Poverty in Scotland 2002*, CPAG 2002, pp162–63 and Appendix 3.

3   For example, conventional 'health' indicators tend to focus on 'negative' statistics (e.g. death rates) or administrative targets (e.g. waiting times), rather than measures of well-being like the connectedness of an area, its environmental quality or the adequacy of local retail facilities.

1 Poverty and low income

1   In 1979, there were 7.1 million people living below the 60 per cent of median low income threshold, compared with 14.2 million at its peak in 1997/98.

2   Except where stated otherwise otherwise, the median income is for Britain as a whole.

3   While official data on low incomes has been collected intermittently since at least 1979, data since 1994/95 has been collected on a consistent and far stronger basis than previously. That is the reason for selecting this as the base year.

4   This condition is needed to guard against labelling as an 'improvement' the situation where all incomes fall but the lowest fall less than the average.

5   Gordon, D., Adelman, L., Ashworth, K., Bradshaw, J., Levitas, R., Middleton, S., Pantazis, C., Patsios, D., Payne, S., Townsend, P. and Williams, J., *Poverty and Social Exclusion in Britain*, Joseph Rowntree Foundation, 2000. The survey provides details on material and social deprivation and exclusion in Britain. Lack of socially perceived 'necessities', such as a washing machine, a fridge/freezer, etc. was one of the tools used to assess the level of deprivation and exclusion.

6   For the purpose of measuring the numbers on low income, 'children' are all those under 16 plus those unmarried individuals between 16 and 18 who are on courses leading to qualifications up to and including Highers.

7   This latter commitment, among the departmental Public Service Agreements, makes it clear that the definition of poverty that applies here is the relative one:

This target will be monitored by reference to the number of children in low income households by 2004. Low income households are defined as households with income below 60 per cent of median, as reported in the annual Households Below Average Income (HBAI) Statistics published by the DSS. HBAI Statistics cover Great Britain. Progress will be reported against the 1998/99 baseline figures and methodology. The baseline is 4.2 million children in low income households after housing costs and 3.1 million before housing costs. The definition outlined above is one of a suite of indicators used when looking at low incomes. HBAI also looks at the number of children in low income households in both absolute and persistent terms. (Her Majesty's Treasury, *Public Service Agreement 2001–04, Technical notes*.)

8   The monetary value of the 60 per cent median depends on the composition of the household. In 2000/01, the weekly values were: single adult: £84; lone parent with one child: £124; lone parent with two children: £156; couple: £153; couple with one child: £193; couple with two children: £225. These figures are *after* housing costs (i.e. rent or mortgage and council tax).

9   It should be noted that these figures pre-date the big rise in the Pensioner Minimum Income Guarantee, from £78 to £92 for a single pensioner and from £122 to £141 for a pensioner couple, which took effect in April 2001.

10   For the four years 1997/98 to 2000/01 taken together, New Policy Institute analysis of the *Households Below Average Income* dataset finds 47 per cent of all minority ethnic people and 50 per cent of minority ethnic children living below the relative low income threshold. Based on a sample of 120 minority ethnic households, the degree of statistical uncertainty surrounding these estimates is ± 9 per cent.

11   Data to help look into this subject of 'low income dynamics' is available for Britain from the annual *British Household Panel Survey*. Since the 1999 'wave', an increased Scottish sample within this survey is starting to yield reliable, Scottish-specific data.

12   Rahman, M., Palmer, G. and Kenway, P., *Monitoring Poverty and Social Exclusion 2001*, Joseph Rowntree Foundation, 2001, Indicator 6.

13   New Policy Institute analysis of ward level data supplied by the Department of Work and Pensions.

14   Key benefits are Income Support (badged as the Minimum Income Guarantee for pensioners), Jobseeker's Allowance, Incapacity Benefit, Severe Disablement Allowance and Disability Living Allowance. It should be noted that it does not include the State Retirement Pension.

15 The index was commissioned by the Scottish Office and is published on the Scottish Executive's website. Postcode *sectors* are made up of all those postcodes sharing all but the last two letters in the full postcode, for example, 'G22 5', 'G34 9' or 'G33 4' which are the three most deprived sectors in that index.

16 Evans, M., Noble, M., Wright, G., Smith, G., Lloyd, M. and Dibben, C., *Growing Together or Growing Apart? Geographic Patterns of Change of Income Support and Income-Based Jobseeker's Allowance Claimants in England Between 1995 and 2000*, The Policy Press/Joseph Rowntree Foundation, 2002.

17 At the end of 2000, Weekly Income Support was worth £41 for a single adult aged under 25 and £52 for one aged 25 or over; £82 for a lone parent with one child and £103 for one with two children; £82 for a couple, £112 for a couple with one child and £133 for a couple with two children; and £78 for a single pensioner and £122 for a pensioner couple.

18 *Client Group Analysis: Quarterly Bulletin on the Population of Working Age on Key Benefits – February 2002*, Department for Work and Pensions, Table 7.6a.

19 Palmer, G., Rahman, M. and Kenway, P., *Monitoring Poverty and Social Exclusion*, 2002, Joseph Rowntree Foundation, 2002, Indicator 4a.

20 *Client Group Analyses Quarterly Bulletin on Population of Working Age*, Department for Work and Pensions, 2002, Table 7.5.

21 An example of this view is to be found in the final evaluation of *New Life for Urban Scotland*, a 10-year regeneration strategy in four low-income housing estates concluding in 1998:

A key issue for regeneration is the high levels and concentration of poverty on these estates. In a superficial sense, it is true to say that the way to alleviate poverty is to raise incomes. But that should not be an objective of regeneration programmes...The appropriate objective for alleviating poverty is the equalising of access to life chances, such as adequate support, employment opportunities, good health, sound education, inclusion in society and good housing...It is not open to area-based schemes to opt for a direct financial approach...The nearest might be those measures that local bodies can take to improve take-up of benefits and services by outreach to excluded groups and individuals. (*Final Evaluation of the New Life for Urban Scotland Programme*, Scottish Executive, 1999.)

2 Employment and education

1 This is not the same thing as saying it has no influence over employment, where its powers over economic development – regeneration of vacant land in areas of high unemployment, improving transport links, etc. – mean that it can certainly influence *where* jobs go.

2 For example: the New Futures Fund aimed at people aged between 16 and 34 provides intensive support for unemployed people suffering from serious disadvantage in looking for work; Community Learning Strategy Partnerships aimed at creating new opportunities for adults seeking help with literacy and numeracy; Training for Work, a national adult training programme, targeted at those aged 25 or over who have been unemployed for at least six months in the last year; and a range of initiative aimed at encouraging higher education and study including the abolition of tuition fees, bursaries and loan entitlements for students from low income backgrounds, means-tested childcare grants for lone parents in full-time higher education and funding made available to the Scottish Higher Education Funding Council to help widen access.

3 These risks are calculated for Scotland-only data, using the same methodology as that employed by the DWP to calculate the risks for Britain as a whole. See: *Households Below Average Income 1994/95 to 2000/01*, Department for Work and Pensions, 2002, Appendix 4.

4 *Ethnic Minorities in Scotland*, Scottish Office Central Research Unit, 1991. Dalton, M. and Hampton, K., *Scotland's Ethnic Minority Community 1991: A Census Summary*, Scottish Ethnic Minorities Research Unit, Glasgow Caledonian University, 1994.

5 Green, F., Ashton, D., Burchell, B., Felstead, A. and Davies, B., 'Are British Workers Getting More Skilled?' in Borghans, L. and Grip, A. (eds) *The Over-Educated Worker? The Economics of Skill Utilisation*, Edward Elgar, 2000.

6 This point was made in a report on social exclusion that pre-dates the Executive: 'the attainment levels of the least qualified fifth of children are rising too slowly and slower than the middle fifth. The learning gap is therefore growing, with the labour market demanding a higher minimum skill level for even relatively low-paid jobs'. McCormick, J. and Leicester, G., *Three Nations: Social Exclusion in Scotland*, Scottish Council Foundation, 1998.

7 This indicator (as Milestone 9) appears within the *Social Justice Annual Report 2001*.

8 For these purposes, Standard Grades 5 and 6 count as 'low', 3 and 4 as 'middle' and 1 and 2 as 'high'.

9 Macrae, C., *Literacy and Community Education*, Scottish Executive, 1998.

10 Croxford, L., *Inequality in Attainment at Age 16: A "Home International"; Comparison*, CES Briefing No. 19, Centre for Educational Sociology, University of Edinburgh, 2000.

11 Croxford, L., *Inequality in the First Year of Primary School*, CES Briefing Paper No.16, Centre For Educational Sociology, University of Edinburgh, 1999.

12 Palmer, G., Rahman, M. and Kenway, P., *Monitoring Poverty and Social Exclusion 2002*, Joseph Rowntree Foundation, 2002, Indicator 12a.

13 Webster, D., *Unemployment: How Official Statistics Distort Analysis and Policy, and Why*, paper presented to the Radical Statistics Annual Conference, Newcastle, 2002.

14 Cited in Bailey, N., Turok, I. and Docherty, I., *Edinburgh and Glasgow: Contrasts in Competitiveness and Cohesion*, Department of Urban Studies, University of Glasgow, 1999.

15 Memorandum from David Webster, Chief Housing Officer, Policy Review and Development, Glasgow City Council. *Third Report of the Work and Pensions Select Committee, 'The Government's Employment Strategy'*, 2002.

16 Memorandum from David Donnison, Emeritus Professor, Department of Urban Studies, Glasgow University. *First Report of the Scottish Affairs Committee 'Poverty in Scotland' Volume 2*, 2000, page 286.

17 Bailey, N., Turok, I., and Docherty, I., *Edinburgh and Glasgow: Contrasts in Competitiveness and Cohesion*, University of Glasgow, Department of Urban Studies, 1999, page 29.

18 See, for example, Webster, D., *Bringing People into Work, Reducing Child Poverty? Working Families Tax Credit and the Geography of Worklessness*, University of Glasgow Department of Urban Studies Seminar Paper, 2001.

19 As reported in the Scottish Executive's Local Area Profiles at http://www.scotland.gov.uk/stats

20 Figures drawn from Webster, D., *Explaining Glasgow's Recent Unemployment Performance: Supply Side or Demand Side?* Glasgow City Housing mimeo, 2000.

21 Kenway, P. and Palmer, G., *What the Poverty Numbers Really Show*, Policy Analysis 3, New Policy Institute, 2002. 'Fully working households' are those where at least one adult is working full time and a second, if there is one, is working at least part time.

22 Findings from the *National Adult Learning Survey*, 2001, show that only 31 per cent of adults with no qualification were engaged in some form of learning, whilst 93 to 95 per cent of those with level four participate in learning.

23 The preferred but unreliable source is the Labour Force Survey. The particular problem with this survey is that only around 25 per cent of interviewees respond to the question on pay, too few to provide a reliable sample. The reliable source of data on pay is the New Earnings Survey. However, because of the nature of this survey, it is believed by the UK government statisticians systematically to under-represent those in low paid, and more precarious occupations.

24 *Poverty and Social Exclusion in Rural Scotland. A Report by the Rural Poverty and Inclusion Working Group*, Scottish Executive, 2001, page 15.

25 Netto, G., Arshad, R., de Lima, P., Almeida Diniz, F., MacEwen, M., Patel, V. and Syed, R., *Audit of Research on Minority Ethnic Issues in Scotland from a 'Race' Perspective*, Scottish Executive Central Research Unit, 2001, §7.9.

26 Burchell, B., Day, D., Hudson, M., Ladipo, D., Mankelow, R., Nolan, J., Reed, H., Wichert, I. and Wilkinson, F., *Job Insecurity and Work Intensification: Flexibility and the Changing Boundaries of Work*, Joseph Rowntree Foundation, 1999.

27 White, M. and Forth, J., *Pathways Through Unemployment: The Effects of a Flexible Labour Market*, Joseph Rowntree Foundation, 1998.

28 Ibid. The research is based on the British Household Panel Survey and is therefore for Britain as a whole.

29 Labour Force Survey, Spring Quarter 2002.

30 Palmer, G., Rahman, M. and Kenway, P., *Monitoring Poverty and Social Exclusion*, 2002, Joseph Rowntree Foundation, 2002, Indicator 27a.

31 Ibid, Indicator 28a.

32 *Ethnic Minorities in Scotland*, Scottish Office Central Research Unit, 1991.

33 Brown, U., *Race, Ethnicity and Poverty*, Briefing Sheet 12, The Scottish Poverty Information Unit 2000. Chaudhry, F., *Race and Poverty in Strathclyde: Issues and Opportunities*, Strathclyde Poverty Alliance, 1996.

34 *Ethnic Minorities in Scotland*, Scottish Office Central Research Unit, 1991. Hampton, K., *The Poverty Experiences of Black and Minority Ethnic Women in Glasgow*, Research Paper Number 11, Series 2, SEMRU, Glasgow Caledonian University, 1999.

35 *Ethnic Minorities in Scotland*, Scottish Office Central Research Unit, 1991.

36 Deakins, D., Majmudar, M. and Paddison, A., *Ethnic Minority Enterprise Development in the West of Scotland*, University of Paisley, 1995.

37 Hampton, K. and Bain, M., *Poverty and Ethnic Minorities in Scotland*, Scottish Ethnic Minorities Research Unit, Glasgow Caledonian University, 1995. de Lima, P., 'Research and Action in the Scottish Highlands', in Henderson, P. and Kaur, R. (eds) *Rural Racism*, Community Development, 1999. Brown, U., *Race, Ethnicity and Poverty*, Briefing Sheet 12, The Scottish Poverty Information Unit, 2000.

38 *Ethnic Minorities in Scotland*, Scottish Office Central Research Unit, 1991. Dalton, M. and Hampton, K., *Scotland's Ethnic Minority Community 1991: A Census Summary*, Scottish Ethnic Minorities Research Unit, Glasgow Caledonian University, 1994.

39 *Ethnic Minorities in Scotland,* Scottish Office Central Research Unit, 1991.

40 Conboy, M., *Still not an issue?* Stirling: Central Racial Equality Council, 1992. Shing, M. and Thornley, E., *Glasgow's Young Chinese: Skills Audit,* Glasgow: The Strathclyde Chinese Coordinating Committee, 1994. *'We regret to inform you...'* Commission for Racial Equality, 1996. de Lima, P., 'Research and Action in the Scottish Highlands', in Henderson, P. and Kaur, R. (eds) *Rural Racism,* Community Development, 1999. Brown, U., *Race, Ethnicity and Poverty,* Briefing Sheet 12, The Scottish Poverty Information Unit, 2000.

41 *New Deal for Unemployed People in Scotland – Statistics to end May 2000,* Scottish Executive Central Statistics Unit, 2000.

42 Conboy, M., *Still not an Issue?* Stirling: Central Racial Equality Council, 1992. de Lima, P., 'Research and Action in the Scottish Highlands', in Henderson, P. and Kaur, R. (eds) *Rural Racism,* London: Community Development, 1999.

43 Modood, T., 'Employment' in Modood, T., Berthoud, R., Lakey, J., Nazroo, J., Smith, P., Virdee, S. and Beishon, S. (eds) *Ethnic Minorities in Britain,* Policy Studies Institute, 1997.

44 *Equal Opportunities and Private Sector Employment in Scotland,* Commission for Racial Equality, 2000.

45 Race Equality Advisory Forum, *Making it Real – A Race Equality Strategy for Scotland,* Scottish Executive, 2001.

46 Ibid.

3 Ill health

1   Based on figures for the 1996 age-standardised all-cause mortality rate for selected European countries (but note that figures are not presented for Italy, Spain or Belgium) in: Hanlon, P., Walsh, D., Buchanan, D., Redpath, A., Bain, M., Brewster, D., Chalmers, J., Muir, R., Smalls, M., Willis, J. and Rood, R., *Chasing the Scottish Effect: Why Scotland Needs a Step-change in Health if it is to catch up with the rest of Europe,* Public Health Institute of Scotland, 2001, page 10.

2   Ibid., page 20.

3   Ibid. and Blamey, A., Hanlon, P., Judge, K., and Muirie, J. (eds), *Health Inequalities in the New Scotland,* Health Promotion Policy Unit and Public Health Institute of Scotland, 2002.

4   Ibid. Mental health is also acknowledged as an issue of concern among minority ethnic people: Netto, G., Arshad, R., de Lima, P., Almeida Diniz, F., MacEwen, M., Patel, V. and Syed, R., *Audit of Research on Minority Ethnic Issues in Scotland from a 'Race' Perspective,* Scottish Executive Central Research Unit, 2001, §5.49.

5   *The Eating Habits of 16–29 Year Olds in Greater Glasgow,* Greater Glasgow Health Board Health Promotion Department, 1997.

6   *For Scotland's Children: Better Integrated Services,* Scottish Executive, 2001.

7   Ibid.

8   Macintyre, S., 'Socio-economic Inequalities in Health in Scotland', *Social Justice Annual Report 2001,* Scottish Executive, 2001, page 117.

9   Pavis, S. and Platt, S., *Health Inequalities: The Major Challenge for the New Scotland,* Research Unit in Health and Behavioural Change, University of Edinburgh, 1998.

10 *Social Justice Annual Report 2001,* 'Indicators of Progress: Definitions, data, baseline and trends information', Milestone 5, page 26.

11 Hanlon, P., Walsh, D., Buchanan, D., Redpath, A., Bain, M., Brewster, D., Chalmers, J., Muir, R., Smalls, M., Willis, J. and Rood, R., *Chasing the Scottish Effect: Why Scotland Needs a Step-change in Health if it is to Catch up with the Rest of Europe,* Public Health Institute of Scotland, 2001, page 8.

12 Paterson, I., 'Geographic and Social Inequalities in Health: The Scottish Picture', in Blamey, A., Hanlon, P., Judge, K., and Muirie, J. (eds), *Health Inequalities in the New Scotland,* Health Promotion Policy Unit and Public Health Institute of Scotland, 2002.

13 Pavis, S. and Platt, S., *Health Inequalities: The major challenge for the new Scotland,* Research Unit in Health and Behavioural Change, University of Edinburgh, 1998.

14 *For Scotland's Children: Better Integrated Services,* Scottish Executive, 2001.

15 Blamey, A., Hanlon, P., Judge, K., and Muirie, J. (eds), *Health Inequalities in the New Scotland,* Health Promotion Policy Unit and Public Health Institute of Scotland, 2002.

16 *For Scotland's Children: Better Integrated Services,* Scottish Executive, 2001.

17 *Health in Scotland 1998,* Scottish Executive Health Department, 1999.

18 Blamey, A., Hanlon, P., Judge, K. and Muirie, J. (eds), *Health Inequalities in the New Scotland,* Health Promotion Policy Unit and Public Health Institute of Scotland, 2002, page 36.

19 *Health in Scotland 1998,* Scottish Executive Health Department, 1999.

20 Ibid.

21 Paterson, I., 'Geographic and Social Inequalities in Health: The Scottish Picture', in Blamey, A., Hanlon, P., Judge, K., and Muirie, J. (eds), *Health Inequalities in the New Scotland*, Health Promotion Policy Unit and Public Health Institute of Scotland, 2002.

22 Ibid.

23 Pavis, S. and Platt, S., *Health Inequalities: The major challenge for the new Scotland*, Research Unit in Health and Behavioural Change, University of Edinburgh, 1998.

24 Paterson, I., 'Geographic and Social Inequalities in Health: The Scottish Picture', in Blamey, A., Hanlon, P., Judge, K., and Muirie, J. (eds), *Health Inequalities in the New Scotland*, Health Promotion Policy Unit and Public Health Institute of Scotland, 2002.

25 Blamey, A. and Muirie, J., 'Health Inequality: Setting the Context', in Blamey, A., Hanlon, P., Judge, K., and Muirie, J. (eds), *Health Inequalities in the New Scotland*, Health Promotion Policy Unit and Public Health Institute of Scotland, 2002.

26 Macintyre, S., 'Socio-economic Inequalities in Health in Scotland', *Social Justice Annual Report 2001*, Scottish Executive, 2001, page 116.

27 Paterson, I., 'Geographic and Social Inequalities in Health: The Scottish Picture', in Blamey, A., Hanlon, P., Judge, K., and Muirie, J. (eds), *Health Inequalities in the New Scotland*, Health Promotion Policy Unit and Public Health Institute of Scotland, 2002.

28 Hanlon, P. , Walsh, D., Buchanan, D., Redpath, A., Bain, M., Brewster, D., Chalmers, J., Muir, R., Smalls, M., Willis, J. and Rood, R., *Chasing the Scottish Effect: Why Scotland Needs a Step-change in Health if it is to Catch up with the Rest of Europe*, Public Health Institute of Scotland, 2001, page 26, Figure 3.

29 Blamey, A., Hanlon, P., Judge, K., and Muirie, J. (eds), *Health Inequalities in the New Scotland*, Health Promotion Policy Unit and Public Health Institute of Scotland, 2002, page 19.

30 Paterson, I., 'Geographic and Social Inequalities in Health: The Scottish Picture', in Blamey, A., Hanlon, P., Judge, K., and Muirie, J. (eds), *Health Inequalities in the New Scotland*, Health Promotion Policy Unit and Public Health Institute of Scotland, 2002.

31 Bain, M., 'Patterns and Trends in Health Inequalities', in Blamey, A., Hanlon, P., Judge, K., and Muirie, J. (eds), *Health Inequalities in the New Scotland*, Health Promotion Policy Unit and Public Health Institute of Scotland, 2002, page 22, Box 4.

32 Information from the Scottish General Registrar's Office shows the rate of mortality of 25-year-olds to be 0.81 per 1000, while the suicide rate for 15- to 25-year-olds is 0.197 per 1000, that is, about one-quarter of the total death rate.

33 Bain, M., 'Patterns and Trends in Health Inequalities', in Blamey, A., Hanlon, P., Judge, K., and Muirie, J. (eds), *Health Inequalities in the New Scotland*, Health Promotion Policy Unit and Public Health Institute of Scotland, 2002.

34 Rahman, M., Palmer, G. and Kenway, P., *Monitoring Poverty and Social Exclusion, 2001*, Joseph Rowntree Foundation, 2001, Indicator 21a.

35 *Scottish Drug Misuse Statistics Scotland 2001*, ISD Scotland, 2001, pages 9–10.

36 *The Eating Habits of 16–29 Year Olds in Greater Glasgow,* Greater Glasgow Health Board Health Promotion Department, 1997.

37 *For Scotland's Children: Better Integrated Services*, Scottish Executive, 2001.

38 Paterson, I., 'Geographic and Social Inequalities in Health: The Scottish Picture', in Blamey, A., Hanlon, P., Judge, K., and Muirie, J. (eds), *Health Inequalities in the New Scotland'*, Health Promotion Policy Unit and Public Health Institute of Scotland, 2002.

4 Quality of life and social cohesion

1 The first wave of Scottish Executive research in May 2001 found that, on average, 64 people were sleeping rough overnight in Scotland and that 500 separate individuals had slept rough at least one night in a particular two-week period. *Social Justice Annual Report 2001,* Scottish Executive, 2001, pages 51–52: 'Indicators of Progress: Definitions, Data, Baseline and Trends Information'.

2 Ibid., pages 30 to 32. Milestone 6 aims to reduce the number of households with children living in temporary accommodation.

3 *Scottish Fuel Poverty Statement*, Scottish Executive, 2002, §3.4.

4 The last comprehensive data source on this subject was the 1996 Scottish House Conditions Survey and the next one – the 2002 Survey – will not be available until next year. Surprisingly, evidence connected with fuel poverty, including even whether the home has central heating, is notable by its absence from the annual Scottish Household Survey.

5 *Scottish Fuel Poverty Statement*, Scottish Executive, 2002, §7.7. The 2006 commitment also extends to all elderly residents in the private sector.

6 *Statistical Bulletin HSG/2001/5 Operation of the Homeless Persons Legislation in Scotland 1989–90 to 1999–00: National and Local Authority Analyses*, Housing Statistics Unit, Scottish Executive, 2001, Table 13d.

7 *Data Compendium 2000/01: Performance Information for Scottish Councils*, Audit Scotland, 2002.

8   DTZ Pieda and System Three Social Research, *Homelessness in Rural Scotland,* Scottish Homes, 2000. This is based on local authorities with population density of less than 300 persons per square kilometre.

9   Scottish Household Survey, 1999 and 2000. New Policy Institute analysis.

10 *Scottish Fuel Poverty Statement*, Scottish Executive, 2002, §4.2.

11 http://www.housing.odpm.gov.uk/research/seh/seh01/download/a1_5xls

12 Netto, G., Arshad, R., de Lima, P., Almeida Diniz, F., MacEwen, M., Patel, V. and Syed, R., *Audit of Research on Minority Ethnic Issues in Scotland from a 'Race' Perspective*, Scottish Executive Central Research Unit, 2001, §2.33.

13 This 'official' definition of rural Scotland is based on local authority areas. Finer grained definitions which excluded towns and cities like Perth and Inverness would show an even more marked lack of social housing in rural Scotland.

14 See, for example, Shucksmith, M., Chapman, P., Clark, G. with Black, S. and Conway, E., *Disadvantage in Rural Scotland : A Summary Report*, Rural Forum, 1994; Shucksmith, M., Chapman, P., Clark, G. with Black, S. and Conway, E., *Rural Scotland Today: The Best of Both Worlds?* Avebury, 1996.

15 Hall, P. and others, *The Containment of Urban England*, Allen and Unwin, 1973. Shucksmith, M., *Housebuilding in Britain's Countryside*, Routledge, 1990

16 Newby, H., *Green and Pleasant Land? Social Change in Rural England*, Wildwood House, 2nd edition, 1985.

17 'The low levels of social housing in rural areas means that provision is generally limited to those regarded as in "priority need" and research suggests that demand considerably exceeds supply. Pressures on the owner-occupied sector are associated with demands from those moving to live in rural areas, the improvement in the road network leading to the potential for more commuting and, to a lesser extent, from the demand for second and holiday homes. The effect of the steady levels of migration to rural Scotland has been to increase house prices, which coupled with the low wage levels of much rural employment, has served to exclude low income groups from the housing market.' Scottish Executive, 2000, page 64.

18 Shucksmith, M., *The Definition of Rural Areas and Rural Disadvantage*, Research Report No. 2, Scottish Homes, 1990.

19 Considerable concern was expressed within rural Scotland about the future loss of social housing in rural areas as a result of the Housing (Scotland) Act 2000, which established a Single Social Tenancy. Concerns that this would open up housing association stocks in rural areas to the right to buy led to amendments to the bill in the Scottish Parliament.

20 Shucksmith, M., Watkins, L., and Henderson, *Attitudes and Policies towards Residential Development in the Scottish Countryside*, Journal of Rural Studies, 1993.

21 Shucksmith, M., *Rural Market Housing Studies*, Scottish Homes, 1990.

22 *Rural Scotland: A New Approach*, HMSO, Edinburgh, 2000.

23 Church of Scotland, *Housing Scotland's People: Report of the Church of Scotland's Independent Inquiry into Scottish Housing*, 1988.

24 The issues surrounding data availability in rural areas are discussed in detail by Copus, A. and others, *Small Area Data Sources for Socio-economic Typologies of Rural Scotland*, Scottish Office Central Research Unit, 1998.

25 The relationship between service provision, deprivation and neighbourhood decline is discussed in Kintrea, K. and Atkinson, R., *Neighbourhoods and Social Exclusion: The Research and Policy Implications of Neighbourhood Effects*, University of Glasgow, Department of Urban Studies, 2001.

26 Duffy, B., *Satisfaction and Expectation: Attitudes to Public Services in Deprived Areas*, CASE paper 45, CASE, LSE, 2000. Duffy argues that the notable additional demand for social welfare services in deprived areas highlighted by his analysis of People's Panel data is very likely to result in considerable extra pressure on provision.

27 See, for example, *Better Communities: Bridging the Gap*, Scottish Executive, 2002.

28 The Better Neighbourhood Services Fund, for example, distributes £90m between 12 authorities with the most deprived neighbourhoods in Scotland, with the intention of improving services through the support of pilot initiatives identified by the local communities.

29 See, for example, Jones, J., Platt, S., Namdaran, F., Brook, C., and Greaves, D., *A Participatory Approach to Developing Community-based Indicators and Measures Relating to Health Improvement: A Feasibility Study*, Heriot-Watt University, 2000.

30 Netto, G., Arshad, R., de Lima, P., Almeida Diniz, F., MacEwen, M., Patel, V. and Syed, R., *Audit of Research on Minority Ethnic Issues in Scotland from a 'Race' Perspective*, Scottish Executive Central Research Unit, 2001, §4.42 and §5.45.

31 While the Scottish Household Survey enables a limited assessment of the differential outcomes for different types of neighbourhood, the Scottish Neighbourhood Statistics project should, over time, provide more detailed information on outcomes at a very small area level. It is of fundamental importance that this information is fully exploited to provide as rich an assessment as possible of the extent to which inequalities are being tackled.

32 See, for example, *Poverty and Social Exclusion in Rural Scotland: A Report by the Rural Poverty and Inclusion Working Group*, Scottish Executive, 2001, page 9.

33 OFGEM, the energy markets regulator, reports that customers not paying by Direct Debit on pre-payment meters pay as much as 10 per cent more in electricity bills, and 20 per cent more in gas bills, than those paying by Direct Debit: OFGEM, *Social Action Plan* Report 2001.

34 'Working Together for Scotland: A Programme for Government' states that the government will 'address financial exclusion including producing a national development strategy for credit unions'. This is part of the overarching strategy to tackle social justice.

35 Bramley, G. and Ford, T., 'Painting a Broader Picture of Local Services' in *CRSIS Annual Review 2001*, Edinburgh College of Art, 2001.

36 Areas shown as most deprived according to the Carstairs and Morris index. The index is composed of four indicators judged to represent material disadvantage: overcrowding, male unemployment, social class 4 or 5 and no car. These four indicators are combined to create a composite score which is divided into five categories, ranging from very high to very low deprivation. It is recognised as a broad measure of deprivation. Data is organised according to postcode.

37 Blamey, A., Hanlon, P., Judge, K., and Muirie, J. (eds), *Health Inequalities in the New Scotland*, Health Promotion Policy Unit and Public Health Institute of Scotland, 2002.

38 *Poverty and Social Exclusion in Rural Scotland. A Report by the Rural Poverty and Inclusion Working Group*, Scottish Executive, 2001, page 11.

39 *Scottish Household Survey Bulletin 6*, Scottish Executive, 2001, Tables 36 and 37.

40 Chapman, M., 'Promoting Financial Inclusion: An Asset Based Policy Approach', in *CRSIS Annual Review 2001*, Edinburgh College of Art, 2001.

41 Palmer, G., Rahman, M. and Kenway, P., *Monitoring Poverty and Social Exclusion 2002*, Joseph Rowntree Foundation, 2002, Indicator 43.

42 'Social Capital could be defined as 'the quantity and co-operative quality of relationships between different groups in society. These may be "bonding" relationships within families and ethnic groups, "bridging" relationships between groups, or "linking" relationships between different social classes.' *Social Capital: A Discussion Paper,* Performance and Innovation Unit, 2002.

43 See, for example, Memorandum from David Donnison, Emeritus Professor, Department of Urban Studies, Glasgow University, *First Report of the Scottish Affairs Committee 'Poverty in Scotland' Volume 2,* 2000 which argues that organisations such as the Glasgow Alliance and the Poverty Alliance are evidence of Scotland's notable spirit of community organisation and participation.

44 Turnout is likely to be influenced by a range of factors, including whether the election is closely contested, any particularly pressing local concerns, the level of local party activism, etc. Background analysis undertaken during the construction of this indicator looked at what would happen to the presentation if account were taken of the closeness of the election in each constituency as measured by the size of the majority. Although this analysis found a clear, inverse relationship between the size of the majority and the turnout, it would hardly alter the rankings shown in the map and supporting graph.

45 *The 2000 Scottish Crime Survey: Overview Report*, Scottish Executive, 2002. New Policy Institute analysis.

46 Ibid., Appendix A7.3.

47 Ibid., Appendix A7.2.

48 *Scottish Household Survey Bulletin 6*, Scottish Executive, 2001.

49 *Scottish Household Survey Bulletin 4*, Scottish Executive, 2000.

50 *General Election Results, 7 June 2001*, House of Commons Research Paper 01/54 (revised edition) Table 22; and *Scottish Parliament Election Results 6 May 1999*, Scottish Parliament Research Paper 99/01.

51 *Assessing the Performance of Partnerships: The Impact of National Policies*, Community Planning Taskforce Working Group 4, 2001.